Breaking the Leadership Bottleneck

Breaking the Leadership Bottleneck

Releasing the genius in the bottle

Paul C. Weaver

Sovereign World

Sovereign World Ltd
PO Box 777
Tonbridge
Kent TN11 0ZS
England

ISBN 1 85240 421 3

Cover design by CCD, www.ccdgroup.co.uk
Typeset by CRB Associates, Reepham, Norfolk
Printed in the United States of America

Dedication

My father and mother who prayed before my birth that I would be a leader in the church; to my faithful and loving wife Jennifer and my delightful children Sally and Joel who have encouraged me, believed in me and supported me sacrificially throughout all my ministerial life. To all those who have stood with me in the churches I have pastored, and to my peers in leadership who have shown confidence in God's gifts in my life.

With gratitude . . .

To those who encouraged me to write this book, and to William Kay, Sally Abel, Ian Winter and my wife, Jenn, who helped me hone the book for publication.

Contents

Foreword

A bottleneck, according to the English Dictionary, is a narrow stretch of road or a junction at which traffic is, or may be, held up. Many of us who travel on roads regularly know the frustration that such bottlenecks bring.

Bottlenecks of course have always existed in all walks of life and the church is no exception. Through the years I have heard leaders lambaste congregations for not being what they should be, inferring that they, the congregation, were a bottleneck that was preventing the world from being evangelised. I have come to realise that this, to a large degree, is not the case and *the number one bottleneck to mission is leaders!* Before you switch off and abdicate your responsibility in this area, let me say right at the beginning that this book is not about knocking leaders, but about transforming and helping them. Most leaders are bottlenecks, but they don't realise it. They are not in a state of rebellion, but rather of ignorance. Many lack proper training and very often are unable to perceive their problem. Breaking the bottleneck does not mean the breaking of leaders, but rather the breaking and removing of wrong concepts held by leaders that serve to keep the people in the pews immature and prevent them from taking the gospel to the lost.

All over the world we have 'congregation congestion' because of bottleneck leaders. Sadly, the church is failing to find its destiny and purpose in the world as it is caught up in the 'ecclesiology jams' of life. This book seeks to lovingly, but firmly, address the problems that we leaders who were trained in the twentieth century face. Each chapter looks at a vital subject that is part of the bottleneck of leadership thinking, each of which must be unblocked if the jam is to be released and the church mobilised and released to reach the world.

It is my humble opinion that the Holy Spirit is working overtime to open the eyes and minds of all Christian leaders to the imperatives of the challenge of a united, trained and resourced church, ready for battle. We have, in the Western world, a window of opportunity that is unique to our generation. If we don't grasp that opportunity now, it will result in a decrease of Christian witness, an enlargement of spiritual darkness, and it will be an insult to the Saviour who redeemed us.

My prayer as you read this book is that God's love for the world will increase in your heart and that you will face the areas of bottleneck in your life, asking God to free you, and through that freedom, to free His body, for service and effectiveness. The challenge is quite simple for each of us in the days that are ahead: Will we be a bottleneck, or a conduit for the purposes of God through His church in the world today?

Author's note

Throughout this book there are questions to answer. These are designed to make the lessons of this book personal to your life as a leader. At the end of each chapter there is an evaluation question that helps to assess your standing in the light of the chapter theme. Please circle the number that best fits you at the time of reading. This assessment can be transferred to the last pages in the book for a simple analysis of your leadership.

SECTION ONE

Paradigm Change

Chapter 1

Paradigm Change

This chapter challenges the leader's perception of the local church and therefore the execution of his or her ministry. The church paradigm that you see and live in determines the way you will shape the local church for which you are responsible. Local churches fall into two broad categories: outward-looking and inward-looking. Jesus only ever made provision for an outward-looking and active church. This chapter will confront your church paradigm and challenge your thinking on how Christian leadership should function.

I was watching a programme on television about modern inventors. As someone who has always been intrigued with invention and creativity I was absorbed with the new inventions being displayed. One that caught my eye was a train that ran on a hosepipe instead of a rail track. Another was a perforated cover for soft drink cans to stop wasps getting into the can and stinging you. Some of the inventors had spent years and invested multiple thousands of pounds developing their bright ideas. Of course, when you are presented with a new way of doing an old thing, you wonder why you had not discovered the obvious before. In fact, sometimes you can invent the new thing, but not believe in it. This was the case with the Swiss Watch Federation who invented the quartz watch. They actually believed that people would continue to want spring loaded watches that you wind up daily. They took their new quartz watch to the World

Watch Fair and displayed it as a futuristic idea. The Japanese realised that this new invention would be a world beater and so went into production immediately, almost finishing the Swiss watch industry.

A *paradigm* in management terms is simply a way of looking at, or doing, something. A new paradigm therefore is a new way of doing something. Hence, the quartz watch was a new paradigm; its purpose was still to tell the time, but by using a different method of watch making. A side issue to observe is this: if you don't adapt to the new paradigm, you will be left behind quicker than you might want to believe.

Today the church is facing an unprecedented challenge of new paradigm thinking. Revelation concerning the church and how it should function in a contemporary world is falling from heaven like a mighty Niagara, but the questions is, who is listening? And more importantly, who has the courage to accept and implement the revelation of the Holy Spirit concerning the new paradigm?

Bill Easum has gone as far as saying, 'It is sheer folly to think that the people who led us well during modernity can give us the same quality of leadership in the post/pre-Christian world.'[1] As much as I understand the sentiments of this statement, I do not believe this has to be the experience of a twentieth-century leader. My own transformation is a living proof of this.

I was raised a PK (Pastor's Kid) in a classical Pentecostal environment. I entered the ministry in the mid sixties and successfully pastored two churches until 2001. In 1993 I co-directed a national evangelistic campaign in the UK called 'The Jim Challenge' (J.i.m. stood for 'Jesus in me'). After working trans-denominationally for eighteen months I returned to the church I was pastoring in Scunthorpe, England, totally disillu-sioned by what I had experienced concerning the ability of the church to make any significant impact upon the society outside its walls. The question began to burn in me: what is church? At that time, not many people were asking that question, in fact there was an unhealthy conviction among church leaders that somehow a great crusade or revival would cure the ills of the church. People travelled the world to experience revival in other cultures. I am sure, in reflection, that all this was part of God's plan to bring us face to face with the real issues of church. For me the question drove me back to the Bible and prayer. Surely, God had left a blueprint somewhere for the church in our century? My quest took me to the New Testament and an in-depth study of the role and function of the church. I read the New Testament through a number of times and found myself confronted, at first, with more questions than answers. Gradually I began to see that the way I had led church historically, was a long way away from how church was supposed to function.

From 1994 to 1996 God brought across my path various leaders who were asking similar questions. Some were ahead of me and others were behind. One of those further along the road was a man called Dwight Smith who has since become a dear friend. He has challenged my concept of church in invigorating ways and he continues to input into my life.

During this period, a book that made me realise I was not alone in thinking about church differently was Ralph Neighbour's *Where Do We Go From Here?*[2] At first I was frightened by the challenge of what I was seeing, because I had no modern reference point from which to examine it. However, key principles and values were taking shape within my being which would transform my understanding of 'church'. I realised I would never again be able to see church in the same light as I had in my ministry up to this point.

To cut a long story short, I began to teach and implement my new understanding in my local church. As you would expect, I made some mistakes, but through those mistakes I realised that this new paradigm needed to come first through revelation in order for people to really grasp it. I have since personally prayed and instructed my intercessors to pray for revelation to come to the people I address.

Revelation is the key to understanding	▶ **Action plan** May I encourage you as a reader to open your heart right now and ask the Holy Spirit to bring to your spirit and mind a revelation of church as our Lord intended it to operate?

I have found that to move a traditional church to the new paradigm requires all of its leaders to see the new paradigm, and from that point it will take up to five years to experience the transformation. There are no quick fixes to this process, but more on that later.

Seeing the new paradigm

Before we go forward I want to make reference to how church has arrived at the point we are at today. If we trace the church through the last two thousand years we will observe that at significant times, certain practices were restored to its operation and beliefs. The great Reformation under Martin Luther regarding *justification by faith* is a classic example. The twenty-first century reflects the rich theological mosaic that the fathers of church history have laid. So it is with the ecclesiology of the church. History holds the clues to the revelation for today.

The book of Ezekiel held revelation for me regarding some of the salient points the Holy Spirit was emphasising again to the church. In particular, chapters 8 and 47 were impressed upon my spirit. In this opening chapter I want to use these two chapters to draw your attention to the very clear picture of the old and new paradigms that Ezekiel unfolds for us.

Whilst the passage in Ezekiel 47 has specific application for the pre-millennialist, I believe we can also find within Ezekiel's revelation a prophetic blueprint for the repurposing of the church today. The characteristics of the pictures shown in Ezekiel speak volumes to current thinking within the church.

Before we consider these paradigms let's remind ourselves of some fundamental hermeneutical principles of the interpretation of Scripture. Scripture can be interpreted in at least four different ways: firstly, the literal historic application for the day when the words were given; secondly, the Jewish-prophetic application, if any; thirdly, the prophetic principles for the church, if any; and lastly, a personal application, where God brings encouragement or direction to an individual.

The following thoughts from the Ezekiel passages will address the principles of truth that I believe the modern church is called to adopt if it is to impact a dying world.

The Ezekiel chapter 8 picture

Ezekiel receives two 'pictures' of the temple through a direct revelation from God. It defines clearly the old and new paradigms of church. The Holy Spirit takes the prophet and places him within the walls of the temple. Ezekiel sees a church that, outwardly speaking, has everything in place, but whose heart is a million miles away from God. He sees hypocrisy, impurity and idolatry. He also sees characteristics within the temple structure which encapsulate the old paradigm church that we need to escape from. These are:

- Building orientated
- Clergy dominated
- Predetermined liturgy
- Inward thinking
- Services limited in duration

Despite the revelation and experience of the first-century church, core Old Testament practice and belief found its way into their structural thinking and practice through Constantine's influence on the church in the third century AD. This basic philosophy and system of operation has been inculcated into every section of the church today. I would estimate that over ninety percent of churches in the Western world find themselves bound in the web of Constantinian structure. We have had a reformation of doctrine, but not of ecclesiology.

Let's expand a little on the five facets of old paradigm church as revealed to Ezekiel. Each addresses an area of church structure that needs to be unlocked in modern church by leaders like you and me. The removal of these hindrances needs to take place within our local churches and filter through our denominational structures.

1. Building orientated

The Bible clearly teaches that the people of God should congregate together for encouragement, teaching and inspiration.[3] Unfortunately, this coming together has, for many, introduced an unbiblical concept of *location* being sacred. The place of gathering has become more important that the reason for coming together. The church, sadly, spends vast sums of money maintaining buildings that have no worth other than housing the people of God for their congregational gathering. This is illustrated by James Doward's article that highlights the cost of building maintenance to the financial arm of the Church of England. In 2003 it cost some £6 million to maintain the upkeep of their cathedrals.[4]

Some of our cathedrals carry inscriptions such as, 'Built for the glory of God'. This was true of the craftsmen who built them, but this statement hides within the cathedral's natural beauty a massive theological error, namely that God does not dwell in material buildings; God dwells in the lives of believers. How sad that through the years so many divisions have arisen in local churches over issues to do with the material building. It must grieve the heart of God. It is also worth pointing out that the act of coming together in congregation was not primarily for the non-Christian, but for believers. I wonder where we got this idea that non-Christians can only be saved inside the church sanctuary?

As long as the church holds the building to be more important than the people, the impact of the church on society will be minimal.

People not buildings	▶ **Action plan** Stop and analyse how much of your life, finance and church operation take place in your building? Is this an acceptable percentage? How can you change this?

2. Clergy dominated

The Old Testament experience of church was totally clergy led. The priests communicated the mind of God to the people and offered sacrifices to God on behalf of the people. The reason for this was that the time of the church's revelation of the priest-hood of all believers had not yet arrived.

The New Testament clearly reveals the importance of leaders, but not at the expense of corporate and individual ministry within and through the body of Christ. The theology of the priesthood of all believers removes the need for Christians to come to God through a priest, or to bring to the priest a sacrifice of acceptance. We all have the same High Priest: Jesus Christ. Leadership is neither more spiritual nor more acceptable to God than the ministry of those who sit in the pew or function in the workplace. Christian leadership is a privilege and has a very clear purpose in the training and equipping of Christ's body the church.

3. Predetermined liturgy
In the Old Testament a person going up to the Temple went to a service that was already predetermined. Only on a few extra-ordinary occasions did anything happen differently, for example, the opening of Solomon's Temple, when the planned pro-gramme was overtaken by the glory of the Lord. I wonder if the worship band were too overjoyed after all their rehearsals came to nothing on the big day?

The New Testament opens the window to a different scenario where nothing is really predetermined in liturgical terms outside of Bible study, prayer and communion – all of which was primarily done in houses.[5] The New Testament church offers a dimension of freedom with clearly defined directives for order that allows spontaneity and participation from everyone present.[6] In all these areas, the purpose was to build up the believer spiritually for service and lifestyle, rather than to pursue a repetitious, predetermined experience of liturgy.

I remember many years ago in Sunderland, UK, a man would regularly come to our church services. I noticed that every time he came he cried, but would leave during the final hymn. I thought God was speaking to him. I suggested to the senior minister that next time the man came, I would make my way to the door before the final hymn and talk to him. This I did the following Sunday. As the man approached me, the tears were running down his cheeks. I said, 'Excuse me sir, you are obviously deeply moved, is there any way in which I can help you?' The man replied, 'Thank you, but I will be alright. I come to the service because of the hymns, they always move me.' After some time talking, I realised that this man was not inclined to respond to the overtures of God's truth, but was content and desirous only of having an experience that was emotional. Hymn music was his thing. For some, this might be hard to take on board, but for others, form and ceremony can bring a sense of continuity and security even in a post-modern world. Having said this, creativity, revelation, and Christian development often come from our exposure to God's ways which are different from ours.[7] No one can read the Old or New Testaments without seeing people that were moved to experience another dimension of God via the unexpected, the unusual and the unpredictable. Jesus Himself was prone to live like this. Although His custom was to go to the synagogue, His practice was anything but predictable. It should be noted that I am not arguing for an abandonment of order or truth, but an expectancy of the extraordinary that is based upon the eternal truth we have come to know.

4. Inward thinking

The Old Testament picture of the church reveals that it was very much an 'in house' thing. The Gentile world outside of the Temple did not see or understand anything of the inner workings of the Temple.

Today, the church has inherited this introverted DNA. The prayers tend to be 'bless me' prayers. The finances are allocated to better seating or new decoration or to some other 'comfort' for the people of God. The world outside of the church comes a very poor second in the priorities of most local churches.

5. Services limited in duration

In the Old Testament people went up to the Temple for worship at certain times each day and at prescribed times during the yearly calendar. Church lasted for a duration – miss the time slot and you missed God.

Historically, leaders have judged the spirituality of their members by the number of times they come to church in a week. This reinforces the old paradigm that the church service is the litmus test of spirituality. The more important question is, what happens in the life of a believer for the other 160 hours in a week?

The Ezekiel chapter 47 picture

Twenty years later, the Spirit takes the prophet to see a totally different scenario. Here we have a glimpse of the new paradigm church. Ezekiel finds himself once again in the Temple, but this time his eyes are directed away from the building to a river.

The prophet follows the river, and in so doing unfolds for us the important differences between the old and new paradigms.

The river endorses the importance of coming together, because the river started in the Temple. The river moves beyond the Temple walls to the world outside and gives us our first glimpse of 'the church without walls'.

Before the river runs beyond the walls, it passes the altar and the outer court. These are important places – they remind us of the place of cleansing and of the demarcation lines of our faith. The church has to move from a sentimental understanding of the cross, back to the stark reality of what it cost Christ to save us. The altar in the temple was a horrific image of God's hatred for sin and the price of redemption. The sacrifices being offered on the altar carried the sounds, smells, and images that can only be summarised as a bloody mess. The church of the twenty-first century cannot substitute the sacrifice of Christ, but must affirm it and build upon this deep and lasting revelation if it is to significantly move forward. The altar brings not only cleansing, but a demarcation line between the behaviour of the church and that of the world outside. The courtyard was that demarcation line.

The river then flows beyond the Temple building, and here comes the challenge to the church and its lifestyle, outside that church building. How far and how deep are we prepared to travel in that river? There are four levels measured out by God.

The first is ankle deep, the second is knee deep, the third is waist deep, and the fourth is too deep to walk in. The first three steps enable the Christian to get out of the river if they don't like it. For too long the church has lived this opt-out lifestyle, with people leaving the church because they don't like what's going on. Unfortunately in the Western world today, there is more transferred growth in the church than real growth from new conversions.

The fourth level in the river is a feet-off-the-ground dimension – a complete abandonment to God; a life where we are totally operating by faith. The significance here is that the current of the river dictates where you go and who you minister to.

Feet on the ground or carried by the Spirit?	▶ **Action plan** Think about your church congregation and where they are in the river of God? What percentage is being carried by the river? How many are only ankle deep? What would change this?

The new paradigm church revealed to Ezekiel has three distinct characteristics. It is:

1. A Kingdom church
2. A church of the supernatural
3. A church that transforms the community

1. A Kingdom church

I was travelling in the USA in 2004 and noticed a challenging billboard on the freeway outside Chicago. It read, *The extra mile is part of our regular route and there are no traffic jams on the extra mile.* If you add up the yardage from the riverside to the middle of the river, it is well into the second mile. Jesus taught in Matthew 5 – 6 that Kingdom living is about going the second mile – going beyond the point of what was expected. 'Religion' only ever takes you the first mile. Christians in the Western world fit God into their personal plans and schedule. They find it very hard to go the extra mile. Business, family and leisure get a better deal than God in most cases.

But leaders can be just as guilty in how they structure their days of ministry. In a recent survey of Evangelical ministers in the UK, it was revealed that most pastors would rather study the Bible than visit the sick; they enjoyed the podium more than the counselling room.[8] The amazing insight of this research was that almost everything that the leader wanted to do as a high priority was placed well down the list by the congregational members. Going the extra mile in helping people is still a problem today. Yet, what an excellent example Christ set for us with His appointment with the Samaritan woman at the well. The Bible tells us that Jesus went 'out of His way' to meet her.[9] Jesus went the extra mile. He practised what He preached.

Nominal or extra?	▶ **Action plan** How does your lifestyle compare with the challenge of Kingdom living? Do you love your space more than people? Where are the extra miles in your life?

2. A church of the supernatural

Ezekiel was confronted with a supernatural river. The intention of God for His people was that they should be a supernatural people. Through the ages they had lost that experience, the Temple had become a place of the *symbolic* rather than the *supernatural*. The power of God to confront the impossible was left in the history of their sacred books. But now the prophet was flowing in a river that was heading for the Dead Sea. There is no more difficult situation on the face of the earth than the Dead Sea. I have been there and floated on its salt-impregnated waters. For this sea to be turned into fresh water would be nothing short of a miracle. The challenge of the Spirit to the church today is to be a people of the supernatural. We must be able to face the impossible circumstances of a degenerated world and see them transformed by the power of the Holy Spirit. Wherever this river goes it brings life. In fact, the further away the river moves from the walls of the church building, the greater the supernatural happening.

Natural or supernatural?	▶ **Action plan** Analyse your ministry and congregation as to the content of the supernatural? If the Holy Spirit left your local church, how much would carry on as normal?

3. A church that transforms the community

The river of Ezekiel 47 is more active in the community to transform it than it is in the Temple building. Listening to an interview on Radio 4 about chaplaincy in a shopping centre in the North of England, I was impressed with the words of one non-Christian being interviewed. He was asked what he thought about having a chaplain in the centre. He replied, 'I am all for it. You don't go to church any more, the church comes to you.' Perhaps his theology wasn't quite right, but he hit a raw nerve. Our message to the non-Christian must be 'the church is coming to you and your community' not 'come to church'. The church flowing in the river experienced the Dead Sea become a Mediterranean Sea, where fish swam and fishing nets hung on the bank of the river, where there were fruit trees growing where the river had flowed, for the healing and sustenance of the people. Barren areas became fertile and hopeless situations were rescued and given meaning. The community was transformed by the river.

This is how the early church operated. Peter and John were in the river before they got to the Temple. As a result of this they were able to give the lame man more than an invitation to a healing service the following week; they were able to give out of what they had, and were, flowing in. This is the new paradigm church. Paul finds himself at Macedonia by revelation[10] and as they went to prayer he frees a demon-possessed woman. It is very interesting that nearly all the miracles in the New Testament took place outside of buildings. In certain parts of the world today, the church is growing more outside of the church walls than within them. People are introduced to the family of God in a church building, only *after* they have become Christians.

The church in the community is what Jesus saw when He said, *'Let your light shine before men that they may see your good works and glorify your Father in heaven.'*[11] Notice Jesus saw the light shining in the house, and in the world before people.[12]

Pew or community?	▶ **Action plan** Look at the programmes of your church to see if they have any impact on the community outside the church? What do you offer them? What changes have been experienced? Sit back and dream about your local church having an impact on your community and let that dream drive you to change.

Two big problems to new paradigm living present themselves: firstly, people of the old paradigm like their well-established comfort zone, and secondly, the leaders of old paradigm churches don't really know how to lead their congregations through the change process. This book is about helping leaders to bring about paradigm change within their local churches and by so doing to break the leadership bottleneck.

In the process of change, the following observations concerning the power of paradigms will help the leader to maintain their equilibrium:

- Paradigm shifters are usually found at the edge of the existing paradigm.
- Always begin the search for the new paradigm while the old paradigm is still successful.
- We see best what we are supposed to see and often manipulate the data to do just that.
- Paradigms held too strongly can lead to 'paradigm paralysis' and your paradigm becomes ***the*** paradigm.
- It is fatal to project the future as a simple extension of the past.
- Paradigm pliancy is the best strategy in times of rapid and turbulent change.
- A new paradigm means that everyone goes back to zero.

Key questions for church leaders

1. What past perceptions stop you from seeing the present?
2. What perceptions about the present keep you from seeing the future?
3. Does your present paradigm allow you to fully minister to the diversity of your congregation and reach the unchurched population?
4. How do your theological paradigms affect your methodological paradigms?
5. Where is your church most vulnerable if the rules change and you go back to zero?[13]

We ask the question, what sort of leader does the church of today require if the ministry of the local church is to transcend the church walls? The following chapters will help any leader who is dissatisfied with the old and hungry for a supernatural church in the community, to learn new ways of leadership that will bring this transformation into reality.

Is your leadership a bottleneck to the new paradigm?

1 ... 2 ... 3 ... 4 ... 5 ... 6 ... 7 ... 8 ... 9 ... 10

Chapter 2

The Leader and Culture

Culture always plays its part in shaping our lifestyle. In different parts of the world and through the centuries, Christian leaders have faced a multitude of different cultures. Consequently, leaders need the wisdom of God to bring evangelism and church planting to bear in such diverse circumstances. Depravity and social issues challenge the twenty-first century leader in an unprecedented way. But the Bible does not change. Contemporary leaders must learn new skills to confront and impact every culture with biblical values.

Culture is a vast field and endless books have been written on this subject. Culture, whether we like it or not, is something that affects all of us, every day of our lives. Very often, however, we are not aware of its influence on us or the church.

The question we must address in this chapter is, how is twenty-first century culture different to twentieth-century culture?

If a paradigm change is needed for the church to positively affect the community outside of its church walls, then the church must understand the culture where it is going to minister.

Culture is: *the totality of its inherited ideas, beliefs, values, and knowledge, which constitute the shared bases of social action.*[1] This definition gives us an important insight into what is inherent in the lives of the people we want to reach with the gospel. Not only does culture shape the views of individuals, but through individuals it shapes the corporate views of groups and communities. Amazingly, most of us don't realise just how much this cocktail of built-in influences shape us.

When Paul walked up Mars Hill he allowed the culture of the context in which he found himself to affect his sermon preparation. He knew the people he would be speaking to were 'religious' people. Their belief system wanted to embrace all deities, a little like Hinduism today. I remember the first time that I visited India, I was asked by a Hindu neighbour of a Christian I was visiting, if I would pray for her. Imagine my delight as I was convinced this was the power of God working through my anointed life! I prayed for her with great faith and articulated the gospel message through my prayer. The lady was radiant and most grateful for my prayer. I came away with a good feeling, until I was told by my interpreter, that she sought only a blessing from yet another god for her life. The fact that she believed in millions of different gods already, had eluded my Western mind. Paul the apostle was a bit sharper than I was. He could see the numerous monuments to named gods on Mars Hill, but noticed one acknowledging the 'unknown god'. It would seem that this community not only crossed their fingers, but their toes as well! Paul therefore began his message by acknowledging their recognition that there was 'something else' beyond human existence – a god, a belief system, an experience. Paul understood their culture and was able to communicate to them that he knew the unknown God they were searching for.

Phil Hill in his book *The Church of the Third Millennium*, says, 'We are living through a revolution. It is not a political upheaval but rather a massive change in the beliefs on which people base their understanding of life.'[2] We could identify this as postmodernism. Phil takes the word 'spiritual' and shows how, for hundreds of years, this simply meant, 'someone close to God'. The twenty-first century meaning has been changed to mean, 'sensitive to the non-rational'. The fact that a person says, 'I'm spiritual' does not necessarily mean they are close to God and on their way to heaven. They might simply believe in the mysterious and prefer to consult with a psychic or astrologist. For the

Christian who is unaware of the change of meaning this can be catastrophic. The twenty-first century, 'I feel' has also changed to become 'what feels good to me is right, whether or not it has a rational explanation'.

Another significant change within Western culture has been the increased importance in experimentation, and of experience. Today, people want to know, 'Have you done it?'; 'Are you a virgin?'; 'Are you into drugs?' This emphasis calls for the church to not only know what it believes, but also to be able to demonstrate its belief with signs and wonders. Twenty-first century society is more vulnerable than ever, because it has replaced its mind with its emotions. How can the church there-fore, best approach such a culture?

During my training as a Christian leader, apologetics was high on the agenda. Today the first port of call in outreach is not apologetics, but probably social action. Society is saying, 'When I feel and know that you care for me I will listen to what you have to say.' It was J. John, an Anglican evangelist, who pointed out in the late nineties that people in the twentieth century had to believe the truth to belong to the church, but today they need to belong in order to believe. J. John was not saying that you could get into the Kingdom of God just by being with Christians, he was saying that people of the twenty-first century need to *feel* and *see* before they will believe.

Twenty-first century people have also been educated differ-ently from twentieth century people. They have been schooled to *research* in order to find the answers to life. They are trained to work in groups to present their projects; to *discover* rather than be lectured; to dialogue and to ask difficult questions. This is why outreach material from the church that embodies discussion and non-threatening interchange finds acceptance among non-Christians. The Alpha courses are a very good example of this approach.

Graham Tomlin raises another important point when he says, 'Contemporary post-modern people are much more sensitised than previous generations to power games and how they oper-ate, and are likely to pick up much more quickly when power is abused by those in authority, whether teachers, doctors, politicians or priests.'[3] In this new culture, reality, integrity and non-pomposity are cool.

On the other hand, one of the unexpected positive outcomes of twenty-first century society in the Western world is its ignorance of Christian belief. When I was growing up in the fifties, we encountered much prejudice to the gospel because most people had been through the church system and rejected it. Today we have a generation of people who are just plain ignorant of the truth concerning Jesus Christ. We cannot assume they know the story of the Prodigal Son or the end to the Nativity. In this sense, post-modern society is wide open to genuine Christianity. Another positive outcome is that this generation wants to *experience life*; they are people who want to get involved as opposed to being just spectators. One only has to look at the growth of such phenomena as Karaoke to see this is true! It means that there is willingness to get involved in the community that did not exist in previous generations. Statistics already show that Christian young people are more aware of social and environmental issues than previous generations were.[4] Their involvement however, is to do with the need they see, rather than conformity to institutional involvement.

Twenty-first century culture is also an inquisitive culture. People are looking for alternatives, willing to try different religions and belief systems to see 'what works'. The church leader must understand the opportunity this affords for the Christian message and by understanding the culture he lives in, he will be able to equip his church to impact the community they are a part of.

Leith Anderson urges the church of the third millennium not to fall into the pit of focusing on its *performance* instead of its *credentials* in its desire to reach society in a contemporary way.[5] In a debate in 2003 in the Anglican Church on the subject of homosexuality, the Bishop of Oxford argued that the prospective gay candidate for a bishopric was a 'gifted man', and therefore should be accepted. But emphasising gift at the expense of character is like launching a ship with a hole, it will not be long before it sinks. Christianity must be more than a good show where goodwill is gained, but lifestyle is left wanting. In the journey of the church from the old to the new paradigm, church leaders must avoid being distracted by the mega-church mentality with their perfected programmes. Some of these churches already have the cracks of subsidence within them. Their programmes have been developed to a very high standard. Money has been invested to raise the quality and ministry of their local church in order for it to have excellence in all it does. The literature, music, building, human resources and so on, speak of success. But a closer inspection into some of these churches, reveals that we are only looking at a beautifully dressed old paradigm. This will not attract the twenty-first century generation for very long. They will see through it and leave.

The church needs to answer the questions the world is asking. It can only do this if it understands the culture and is in a place where it can hear the questions being asked by the world. Peter Corney, an Australian Anglican, said, 'People have changed address and unless we work out where they are we will fail to communicate with them.'

Getting the church to engage in the process of 'trans formational church', moving from the old to the new paradigm, is not easy. George Barna has verbalised a similar challenge to American Christianity, and he also offers three starter answers:[6]

- We must motivate people to pursue, embrace and live according to a biblical world-view.
- We must allow the church to be led by the people whom God has called and anointed for the task – that is, leaders.
- We must develop new forums and formats through which people will experience, understand and serve God.

This of course presupposes that leaders and congregational members can see their biblical responsibility for reaching the people of our communities for Christ. Peter Brierley says, regarding the challenge of leadership and the third millennium, 'Our calling is to find out what Jesus is doing and join Him in doing it.'[7] To do this, we must resist old paradigm leadership at all costs. So what then must be done?

The hard cultural challenges facing the church today require the acceptance, sooner rather than later, of a different type of leadership in the church. The Christian message is a life and death matter. Unless we communicate this message vibrantly and relevantly, this generation will die outside of a personal experience of God's grace in their lives.

To face or not to face the cultural question, is the question	▶ **Action plan** Make a parallel list of how you do things in the church with the way things are done in the community. What lessons can you learn from this exercise?

Is your leadership a bottleneck to penetrating twenty-first century culture?

1 ... 2 ... 3 ... 4 ... 5 ... 6 ... 7 ... 8 ... 9 ... 10

Chapter 3

The Leader's Mind

The way we think has a strong influence on the way we act. Everyone has their mind shaped by their upbringing. The challenge of this chapter is to assess whether the influence of our upbringing harmonises with the mind of Christ.

The greatest restriction to progress in life is the mind-set we hold. Our perspective on life is our reality, whether or not it is true. Most of us live in a very tightly defined box that the rest of life has to be filtered through. We are limited by our inability to live by a positive set of values that allow flexibility in our thinking and leadership without losing truth.

Most of the challenges that I have faced in personal change, as well as those I have faced at local and national levels, have been to do with the mind. I am amazed sometimes at the entrenched messages of opposition to change, that my mind sends out at times.

I was challenged by a brilliant lecture I heard from Alan Chambers, the British explorer who was the first man to reach the North Pole unaided. His plan was to eliminate eighty percent of potential problems before he commenced the journey, and he used the following phrase to describe the many situations that he had confronted in the five-year preparation for his expedition: 'Never put your body where your mind has not already been.' Of course as Christian leaders we would want to add something to that statement in order to understand our tripartite nature and the importance of our spirit. Perhaps we might say, 'Never put your body, where your mind and spirit have not already been.' I fear that we Christian leaders are good at putting our bodies where our minds have never been and where the Spirit has never led us. Our mind is important to our actions.

A Christian leader has to learn early on in ministry that there are certain values and principles that do not change; they are non-negotiable and are the springboard for enduring success. Leaders must also learn that the creative power of the Holy Spirit in their lives will lead them into unpredictable areas of Christian leadership and understanding – which is in total harmony with the biblical history of God's servants in the Old and New Testaments. The key to a balanced and effective ministry is to hold a correct mind-set and view of life.

I hope the following will help you craft your future 'outside the box', without compromising the truth you believe in. I would like to suggest that there are five critical elements to a new paradigm mind-set:

1. Stay fresh in God
Most leaders get discouraged when their circumstances in life overwhelm their experience in God. Isaiah the prophet reminds us that it is possible to keep going – we can *'run and not be weary'* and *'walk and not faint'*.[1]

There is no vacuum, emptiness or lacking in God. He is our all sufficiency. He is the antidote to our emptiness, fatigue and discouragement. But He is also the inspiration behind our creativity and perceptions of life. As I look back over my life, the worrying times have been the times when my relationship with God has been at its weakest. The Christian leader must never forget that their earthly good is only as strong as their heavenly mindedness.

Fresh or stale?	▶ **Action plan**
	There is no pressing circumstance more important than your daily communion with Father. How is your prayer life? Improve on what you have; don't let the enemy condemn you. How are you going to improve?

2. Live by principles and values

The trap most leaders fall into is to reduce a liberating truth to a mechanical, lifeless expression of that truth. This is where Judaism found itself when Christ came to planet earth. The ministry of Christ operated in pure unadulterated truth. Jesus was able to transcend the cultural and religious world He lived in because the truth that He brought was lived out by *principle* rather than *rite*. Here are three examples: Christ's values transcended tradition in John 4:1–29; Christ's values transcended race in Luke 10:30–37; and Christ's values transcended the law John 8:3–11.

As a Christian leader it is important to learn this skill. Your values do not only determine what you believe, but they also allow you flexibility in how you exercise those values. Compromise is the sacrifice of truth for political or social peace or gain. Living by values enables you to be uncompromising with the truth, but adventurous and unconventional, when required, in the execution of the truth you believe in. This mind-set enables the leader to live unshackled.

Steven Sample talks about *thinking grey and free* in his book *The Contrarian's Guide to Leadership*. His basic argument goes against the quick and decisive decision making that is normally propounded by books on leadership. Sample argues, 'for leaders, judgments as to the truth or falsity of information or the merits of new ideas should be arrived at as slowly and subtly as possible – and in many cases not at all'.[2] The mind, if allowed, has the ability to sift a number of options as well as arriving at creative ways of delivering the truth unadulterated. Authentic creativeness is best manifested on the foundations of sure values and principles.

Values or traditions	▶ **Action plan** Analyse why you do what you do. Does your ministry keep people in check or does it enable people to live out the truth? Are you an example of the truth you espouse?

3. Put missiology before ecclesiology

Martin Kahler said, 'Mission is the mother of theology ... Theology began as an accompanying manifestation of the Christian mission.'[3]

Every Christian leader in pastoral ministry enters into an environment of structure. The theological word for this is ecclesiology. The problem for most leaders is the demand by the system to conform to the structure. My good friend Alan Hewitt calls this, 'the grinding wheels of conformity'. These wheels have a way of killing new ideas by making them bow to the altar of intransigence. This of course guarantees safety, but negates true growth or creativity. It says in effect, 'We can only do mission if it fits into our structural pattern.' This is like putting the cart before the horse. Liberated leadership looks at the need first and then finds a structure for reaching that need. Jesus did this when He healed the man on the Sabbath day. He focused on the mission before the letter of the law. Early Christianity is all about this kind of liberated leadership.

The strategy of Christ was always in the *direction* of mission, not in the *method* of mission. His words in Acts 1:8 effectively opened the doors on the front step of the Jerusalem church for it to reach the furthest point of the globe. The early leaders went in the power of the Holy Spirit and with the truth of Christ's teaching. They put mission before ecclesiology and used the authority of Christ in their lives to bring about miracles: 'Such as we have, in the name of Jesus rise up and walk.' In this respect, George Lings makes a telling observation regarding the lack of church planting in the UK, 'Ecclesiology was sidelined as self-evident or buried under corporate individualism. Unthinking replication of congregational forms resulted, without due attention to ecclesial alternatives or the mission context. But passionate evangelism needs agile and committed ecclesiology.'[4]

The question is often asked, what came first the chicken or the egg? The answer is simple, the chicken, according to Genesis chapters 1 – 2. What must come first in the practice of Christian service, mission or structure? The answer has to be mission. Structure alone will never birth significant mission.

Leadership must therefore discipline its ministry to operate in the domain of mission if it is to stay relevant to the challenge of Christ's commission.

Mission or maintenance?	▶ **Action plan** Look at your mission programmes to see why you do them. What restrictions are in your structure that stops you doing other mission programmes?

4. Don't get stuck in a model or programme

The twentieth century has taught me the danger of getting stuck in a programme or model of church life. There is no single church model or pattern in the New Testament. Beware when you hear the words, 'This is God's model.' If you believe that, you will find yourself entrapped sooner than later in the box of that model. Programmes and models are delivery structures to help us experience some facet of Christian truth. But because the church is ever discovering its fuller purpose, it will always be discovering or rediscovering certain aspects of its purpose that it needs to embrace.

To stay focused, we need to ask of any programme or church model being offered to us, 'What is this programme/model seeking to teach me?' In every new programme or model there is an emphasis of the Holy Spirit that the church must grasp. We could illustrate this from the twentieth century by observing the following that has or is taking place: the restoration of the gifts of the Holy Spirit; the restoration of team ministry; the restoration of worship; the restoration of apostolic and prophetic ministry; the restoration of small group meetings; the restoration of the priesthood of all believers; the restoration of first century ecclesiology. Each of these important areas of emphasis could easily become an expression of 'boxed church' if they are not received with a wider understanding of church apart from the facet being examined at that time.

The process of God's dealings with us is simple. God moves in our lives by revelation. One revelation leads to another. It is like walking into a very large castle with many rooms. If you were to stay in one room only and say 'This is the castle,' you would not only be denying yourself the experience of the whole castle, but also magnifying the importance of your discovery beyond its intended purpose. Each revelation is like another door opening onto another room of the full plan of God for His church. As we pass into a new room, we do not deny the experience of the previous one, but understand that it was an access point to the next revelation. Each room gives us a better understanding of *all* the rooms. Even if we think the room we are in now is *very important*, time will provide us with a correct view of its proper place within the totality of the church.

Sometimes when I am lecturing on this subject I produce a power-point illustration. On the screen is a Jack-in-the-Box. The Box and the Jack springing out are all in proportion. Stars and rainbows are coming out of the Box and Jack is happy and declares these words to the world, 'I have found the church model for growth!' The next slide shows a picture of Jack ten years later. The Box has grown and Jack is dwarfed in the Box and a feeble voice sends out this telling cry, 'Will someone please get me out of the Box?'

Revelation or model?	▶ **Action plan** Examine your church model to see the things it has delivered for you, but also the areas that may be missing. Ask yourself, have I been in this model too long?

5. Think tomorrow, live today

The Christian leader must feel at home in two places at the same time – the practicality of the present and the challenge of the future. If a leader inhabits either of these exclusively, he will be left with either a maintenance ministry or a dream ministry that is going nowhere.

The questions leaders need to continually ask themselves, if they are to maintain this balance are:

- Have I implemented the lessons learned from the last revelation?

- Do I know where the next revelation is taking me?
- What is the pace of the journey to the reality of the next revelation?

It is amazing how many leaders live in one or the other of these two domains. Very often the ministry of the pastor is only in *the now*, whereas the ministry of the apostle is only in *the future*. Some time ago I was watching a documentary on Richard Branson and his investment in one of the railway companies in the UK. His ability to see the future, while still living in the present was illustrated by the placing of his Virgin logo on old rolling stock. This was a gamble on his part, because the Virgin logo stands for innovation and new thinking. The railway in 1996 represented anything but that. But Branson could see into the future: new rolling stock, faster trains, and comfortable seats. He had to live in the real world of the now, but let his dream transform the old stock into new stock and so confirm the value of the Virgin logo.

Sometimes we have to run with programmes that are less than we desire, but they must all have the marks of something better in them – something that will eventually evolve into the realisation of the dream we had for the future.

	▶ **Action plan**
Today and tomorrow	Where does your gift operate most comfortably, in today or tomorrow? Imagine your church in five years time. What does it look like? Will it be the same as it was five years ago? Does this tell you anything about your leadership?

Is your leadership a bottleneck to the thinking of the local church?

1 ... 2 ... 3 ... 4 ... 5 ... 6 ... 7 ... 8 ... 9 ... 10

Chapter 4

The Leader's Calling

Many leaders hold their position whilst failing to lead in the way God intended. This chapter helps leaders to align with their calling by addressing five foundational areas of true Christian leadership.

To understand church in the third millennium we must never forget that there are two clear roles that people occupy within it. There are those who are leaders and those who are followers. Jesus endorsed this in John 10 when He talked about the sheep knowing the voice of their Shepherd.

We know that leadership equals influence. Walter Wright said, 'Leadership is a relationship of influence that connects the character of the leader with the culture of the community and ultimately impacts the bottom line productivity of the organisation.'[1] It is true to say that each one of us influences other people in varying degrees, whether or not we are leaders. A leader however, is a person who influences large groups of people to accomplish a specific purpose.

This chapter addresses the call of the leader in the context of the fivefold ministry gifts of Ephesians 4:11. We know that there are leadership roles other than these and we will address some of those roles later on. I am looking at this aspect of leadership first because it is quite clear that among the many different expressions of leadership in the New Testament, there were some who were clearly 'leaders of leaders'. These were special leadership gifts given by God to the universal church. Paul defined these gifts as apostle, prophet, evangelist, teacher and pastor. These are positions with authority delegated by Jesus Christ and represent a leadership calling given to few. This leadership is to do with more than personal ability, gift or learning – it is a divine calling to a role that a person cannot assume for themselves.

At the beginning of this chapter, let me make a few observations concerning these gifts. They are God appointed, recognised through their function in the church and needed for all the generations of the church on earth. They are to be honoured by all in the church as they are the equippers of the church for its ministry, and they are used by God with different emphases and at different times for specific purposes.

These gifts have a mystical dimension of effectiveness that defies human interpretation. These gifted people may not be the most talented or even be the most spiritual, but they have within their God-ordained calling a power to effectively equip the church for ministry that transcends the logical restraints of management definition. Colin Powell defines leadership as, 'The art of accomplishing more than the science of management says is possible.'[2] If this is true in the secular world it is most certainly true in respect to Ephesians 4:11 leadership.

Who are you?	▶ **Action plan** From Ephesians 4:11 write down which gift(s) you are to the church. Then write down what you are not. Now spend some time thinking about this in practical terms.

There is a clear destiny in the call of Ephesians 4:11 leaders. They are not accidents or people who have aspired to their calling. They are God-given and therefore have a clear mandate from heaven. Their destiny has within its vista a clear purpose. This is something I came to realise both in my new understanding of leadership at a local level and in my national role as General Superintendent of Assemblies of God in Great Britain and Ireland. What is the purpose of our leadership? We could respond with many relevant answers, but at the core of our purpose is our mission to those who have not yet believed in Jesus as our sacrifice for sin. Because the church has lived for itself for so long, its mission heart has been lost and is pacified through the occasional evangelistic crusade or programme of evangelism. Most Christians do not enjoy sharing their faith and are generally relieved when any evangelistic mission is over.

When we look at Christ's final words to His disciples, 'Go into the entire world and preach the gospel ...'[3] we see a Saviour pregnant with mission and purpose for the church. The church is clearly sent to the multitudes of people living outside the knowledge of Christ's love. Unfortunately, leaders have turned the command of Christ to 'Go' into an invitation to 'Come'. Through this unforgivable change of emphasis, leaders have made it almost impossible for the unbeliever to see the glory of God. The church unfortunately, is in hiding.

When I began to see this error of the church, I determined to change the reason for our being as a local church, and later as a denomination, by spelling out the 'purpose' of the church afresh. In my local church I placed in beautiful writing two large declarations at the front of the church building. The one on the left read, 'The purpose of our church is ... ' The one on the right read, 'The aim of our church is ... ' When I challenged our denomination to change, I gave them the following purpose: *The purpose of Assemblies of God is to give every man, woman and child the opportunity of understanding the gospel and to provide a church where they can grow and develop in ministry for the glory of God.* There are three important things to observe from this mission statement of purpose. Our mission is:

- to reach everyone with the gospel,
- to provide churches where Christians can be equipped, grow and develop into functional servants of God,
- to release the equipped congregation to the world in mission.

In simple language, this means growing a mobilised church.

Such a mission purpose will radically affect the leadership function of the local church. Leadership is at the centre of twenty-first century paradigm church. Leadership has always shaped history for good or evil. In the secular world the names of Napoleon, Abraham Lincoln, Adolph Hitler, Winston Churchill, and Nelson Mandela spring to mind. Biblically speaking, Moses, Joshua, David, Peter and Paul are heroes that are referred to continually. Church history also has its giants: Martin Luther, John Wesley, General Booth, William Carey and Billy Graham to name but a few. Leadership often becomes a window of illumination to the church as a whole revealing what it is that God wants doing. If those windows are shuttered, the church will grope in the darkness, but if those windows allow the light of God's revelation to shine through, the church will know progress. Breaking the leadership bottleneck is all about this process.

The leader's calling can be expressed in the following five words according to the Great Commission:[4]

1. 'Go'

The vision of Jesus was for proactive leadership. The Greek word for 'go' simply means, *to proceed from one place to another.* This command is endorsed by Jesus in Matthew 10:7; 22:9; 28:7. Can it be that most leaders are standing still addressing the same people over and over again going nowhere?

In the command to 'go' is also the command to 'teach'. In Matthew 28:19 Jesus' command is translated as 'teach all nations'. The concept of teaching is mentioned twice in the great commission: in Matthew 28:19 the word 'teach' is *matheteuo* meaning 'to be a disciple'. This word can be interpreted as either 'to instruct' or 'to make a disciple'. In the Amplified Bible the word 'teach' is translated as 'make'. How do you make disciples? How do you make anything? You make things by planning a process and by knowing what the end product will look like. You make things by being in contact with and shaping the raw material.

Vine tells us that the word for 'teach' can be translated as, 'being a disciple of a person' or 'one who has been made a disciple'.[5] Either way the process of making a disciple was envisaged by Jesus. Leadership can only have New Testament credibility where disciples are being made.

	▶ **Action plan**
Where are your disciples?	Make a list of those you have personally discipled above and beyond the input you have given from the platform.

In Matthew 28:20 the word for 'teaching' is the word *didasko*, meaning 'to teach'. Public teaching is envisaged more in this word. We talk today about a didactic approach, meaning to educate, instruct. This word is linked, however, to obedience, *'Teach them to observe all things that I have commanded you . . . '* Here we have not only a public declaration of truth, but an expectation of conformity. There are many illustrations in the New Testament from Ananias and Sapphira in Acts chapter 5, to the people of God being called to account in respect to their obedience to the taught word in Revelation chapter 3.

Conversion does not make you a disciple of Christ. It may give you the gift of salvation, but it does not make you a disciple. Jesus says, *'If you abide in my word, you are my disciples indeed'*, not 'if you give mental accent to belief' only. Discipleship does not automatically happen. If it did, the world would have been impacted for God much more than it has. No, as leaders, we need to make disciples. Are you making disciples? God has planned the essential ingredient of Ephesians 4:11 ministries to be the catalysts of the discipling process. During my travels in the early nineties I found that in the UK less than 20% of churches had any form of discipleship material for new converts.[6]

The Apostle Paul describes the work of a mature disciple (spiritual person)[7] as someone who helps the fallen back to maturity, carries the burden of someone who has fallen for a while, challenges personal conduct, hands back responsibility to the recovered with the expectation of fruitfulness, and contributes to the support of the person who is discipling them.[8]

The idea of shaping a person's life is also enforced through the words taught in Galatians 6:6 which can be interpreted as mentoring, shaping, and making. (The illustration in Galatians obviously refers to more than simply a podium teacher.)

Returning to the commission of Christ we can see a further characteristic of making disciples in the verse containing the command to baptise.[9] The leadership that Jesus commissions in this passage is not a maintenance leadership, but a progressive leadership that actively seeks new converts and does not wait years for their water baptism. Water baptism is the first stage in the discipleship track. It is disturbing that many churches do not have any baptismal services, or have them very infrequently. We made a decision some years ago that we would baptise every month, even if there was only one person for baptism. It's amazing how people rise to the occasion when confronted with the opportunity on a regular basis!

Please observe Christ's encouragement for leaders who will face their responsibility in this matter: *'I am with you.'* Not, *'I will be with you'*, but *'I **am** with you.'*

Baptised or not?	▶ **Action plan** List the number of people that have been baptised in water in your church during the last two years. What is this number saying about your ministry?

2. 'Stay'

In the first command of Christ to 'Go' we saw an apostolic dimension; in this second word 'Stay', we see a pastoral element.

This idea of *staying* is endorsed by Christ in John 10:11–13 as an authentic mark of a true pastor:

> *'I am the good shepherd. The good shepherd lays down his life for the sheep. The hired hand is not the shepherd who owns the sheep. So when he sees the wolf coming, he abandons the sheep and runs away. Then the wolf attacks the flock and scatters it. The man runs away because he is a hired hand and cares nothing for the sheep.'* (NIV)

We are called by God not only to *go*, but also to *stay*. Our going is in the proclamation of the gospel. Our staying is in caring for the sheep.

The Ephesians 4:11 gifts have within their diversity a comprehensive ministry that can execute leadership for every aspect of church life. In this John 10 passage is an illustration of two kinds of leaders. The first is illustrated by Christ Himself as the good shepherd. The significant point to observe about the 'called' is the personal sacrifice that calling demands. Jesus did *all* the paying. Stop and think about that in the present climate of Christian leadership.

In the early sixties I left a job as a buyer in an engineering firm. At the time my colleagues could not understand why I was leaving a well-paid job for employment with apparently no secure future. I seemed in their eyes to be the loser. There is a price to pay in Christian leadership; the call of God requires it.

The second kind of leader is the one who is in it for the money. The test of authenticity is the tough times. When these difficult times come, those who are called, stay, the person who is only in the ministry for the career, salary or position, runs away. Jesus saw that true leadership was there for the long haul. When it gets tough, we do not quit. The Contemporary English Version translates Paul's determination to stay in 2 Corinthians 4 with this recurring phrase, 'We never give up'. One of the marks of God's calling is found in the ability of the leader to survive the storm.

For a paradigm change to take place in the lives of a congregation it requires leaders to experience change within themselves, and *to stay*.

To go or stay	▶ **Action plan** How long have you been a leader in your local church? Has this duration contributed anything to the developing of disciples in your church?

3. 'Equip'

When I was a young minister, my interpretation of Ephesians 4:11–12 reflected the commonly held view that the leaders of the church were the equipped ones and that the congregation stood in awe of such gifting. This misconception led not only to the 'one-man band' syndrome that bound the twentieth century church, but also to the practice of a clergy/laity divide. This view totally ignored the practical out working of the priesthood of all believers.

Since the 1980s however, we have come to see a different interpretation of this verse. Ephesians 4:12 illuminates the call of all leaders to equip and '... *prepare God's people for works of service* ... ' The Amplified version expresses this revelation well:

> 'His intention was the perfecting and the full equipping of the saints (His consecrated people) [that they should do] the work of ministering towards building up Christ's body (the church), [That it might develop] ... '

And in the NIV verse 16 continues:

> 'From him the whole body, joined and held together by every supporting ligament, grows and builds itself up in love, **as each part does its work.**'

Here an engagement is given, through God-given expertise, to the process of developing every child of God for the work of the ministry. The gifts in verse 11 impart expertise to the people in verse 12. Here is a vital key in understanding church in the new paradigm. The leader recognises that their task is to see, develop, and release the God-destiny in the lives of every believer, or put another way to see the genius in the bottle (the body). Dwight Smith put it like this, 'Whatever God is going to do through all of Christ's people in the world, He is going to do through leaders who empower his people as their first priority, and as more important than their own giftedness.'[10]

In the equipping of Christ's body is also the necessary releasing process. Many leaders may have put energy into training, but find it difficult to release or employ those they have trained. Mark's coverage of the Great Commission[11] catches the leader's role in mobilising the body for service. These first apostolic leaders had a call 'to preach the good news to everyone in the world and to baptise believers'. The interesting observation is what kind of followers this produces: a dynamic mobilised body in service. Mark records, that the '**people who believe will, do** wonderful things: **they will** force demons out, **they will** speak new languages, **they will** handle snakes and drink poison and not be hurt, **they will** also heal the sick through the laying on of hands.' The work was not to be exclusively through the apostles, but the believers.

The role and function of the body of Christ cannot be underestimated. Ephesians 4:11 gifts are equipping and releasing agents for the body. Any leadership that does not see this aspect of the Great Commission will restrict the work of the ministry to leadership alone and fail the purposes of God in the church.

Since teaching these principles into the local church I have increasingly observed that new converts are being won to Christ directly through the ministry and through people's encounters in their workplace, community and home.

Who's doing the work?	▶ **Action plan** Count the number of people in your local church who are exercising the works of Mark 16. Commit yourself to see a change from the few to the many in this area of operation.

4. 'Build'

Our fourth element, 'build', is found in 1 Corinthians 3:1–15. This section of God's Word brings together the importance of leadership working together. I have called this, *diversity in harmony*. This is a synergistic expression that reveals the potential of a diverse yet united group of people working together. They will accomplish more together than the sum of each individual's efforts.

Unfortunately, the context of 1 Corinthians 3 is one of carnality. There was a cancerous obsession with personality, a form of cultism, which was dividing the church. People were more interested in following personalities than enjoying the blessing and enrichment that many different kinds of leaders can offer. This problem is in the church today. In society we live in a culture where people are venerated to celebrities and superstars; the church unfortunately is no better. But the power of God is not in the personality, but in the gift within that individual. To follow a leader because we prefer their personality, ministry or gifting, is idolatry of the first degree.

It is important to observe that Paul's counsel in this situation was to focus on the maturity of the body of Christ. He saw diversity of leadership as an instrument of God to bring different aspects of tooling to the great task of building the body of Christ and evangelising the world.

Similarly, when a fine piece of furniture is to be crafted, it's no good just *talking* to the wood. You need to apply your skill by the use of good tools, the saw, hammer, chisel, screwdriver and ruler. Each tool needs to make its mark if the wood is to change. So it is with each of the Ephesians 4:11 gifts. They are like tools in a carpenter's chest, each one is different, but all are needed to build the church. God the giver picks the gift (tool) he wishes to use to perfect His body, the church.

Paul makes another powerful point in 1 Corinthians 3:5 when he highlights the truth that we are all ministering servants, each with a task. In the picture of sowing and reaping, Paul is the planter, Appollos the sprinkler, and so on, but God is always the one that gives the increase. Each of us in our leadership roles must rest in the fact that we all have special endowments of gift (v. 10) and all those gifts are equal (vv. 8–9). None of us have anything to be proud about, and none of us are better than each other in the sight of God, we just have a job to do. Understanding these principles enables us to both clarify our calling and harmonise with those other wonderful gifts God has given to His church.

Today's Christian leaders must understand that their gifting is one of many that are serving the construction of the church. Jesus said, *'I will build my church.'*[12] None of us mere mortals owns the church. It is not ours, nor ever will be. It belongs exclusively to Christ. We must not magnify our part in the building process, we must admire the whole. Our calling then is to use our gifting alongside that of others to the glory of Christ.

Is it me or us?	▶ **Action plan** Do you privately enjoy the limelight of your position? What do you really feel about other gifted people around you? Who are you really building for?

I know this is easier said than done, but without this expression of unity, our ministry will rob the eternal purpose of God in the world.

5. 'Mentor'

The difference between discipling and mentoring is probably not in its purpose but in its application. Mentoring is generally done on a one-to-one basis, where discipling can be done in a small group.

> 'A mentor is simply someone who helps another person to learn something that he or she would have learned less well, more slowly, or not at all if left alone. Mentors are learning coaches – sensitive, trusted advisors ... we are fellow travellers on this journey towards wisdom.'[13]

Walter Wright uses the excellent metaphor of the karabiner from mountaineering to illustrate the mentoring process. The karabiner is the clip that ties a mountaineer into a climbing rope. Being 'roped up' is about tying your life to another.[14]

Mark Millar illustrates this tying together when he unpacks the role of the mentor in his book, *The Secret*. The book opens with an astonished young leader being confronted with the disarming words of his mentor at their very first meeting, 'How can I serve you?' Millar later defines the role of the mentor as a servant and uses the word 'serve' as an acrostic.[15]

See the future
Engage and develop others
Reinvent continuously
Value results and relationships
Embody the values

Mentoring must be at the centre of our leadership calling. The word 'mentor' can be illustrated by many passages of the New and Old Testament, but I have chosen to limit our thoughts to 1 Timothy 4 and 2 Timothy 3. In these chapters Paul addresses the mentoring of younger leaders. Paul is passing on what he has learned to the next generation. He is determined not to carry his wisdom and experience to the grave to be simply boxed up in a coffin; unfortunately this has been the experience of too many church leaders historically.

We see Paul mentoring the young man Timothy on the job, via example, practice, letters, directives and praise. In these two chapters alone Paul addresses the following important subjects: personal spiritual development; social skills; physical health; ministerial responsibility; and family matters. Timothy was not left to go it alone.

One of my greatest personal joys as an older leader is to sit down with younger leaders and encourage them in what they are doing, to learn from them and to draw out of my experience of leadership from the sixties to the present day and pass it on. The Bible continually illustrates the passing on of the baton from generation to generation. Solomon was wiser because of the input into his life of his father David.

When I handed over the senior leadership of the church in Scunthorpe, England in 2001, I was able to hand the church over to a team of leaders who were all home-grown, each quite individual, yet each carrying the wisdom and experience of my years in leadership. Because experience was shared, I now see my life in them in many different ways, and this is very gratifying. Of course this does not mean that they know everything and does not negate times when they get it wrong, but there is a foundation of knowledge that is in them whether they recognise it or not.

Gordon Shea described mentoring as, 'a developmental caring, sharing and helping relationship where one person invests time, know-how and effort in enhancing another person's growth, knowledge and skills responding to critical needs in the life of another person in ways that prepare that person for greater performance, productivity or achievement in the future'.[16] This reason alone should excite any leader to engage in the mentoring process.

Your calling is to mentor others. This does not mean that you insist they become like you. Mentoring is not cloning, it is allowing your reservoir of wisdom and experience to become a place in the lives of the young that they can draw from when facing their challenges in life.

Coffin or communication?	► **Action plan** Write down the names of the people you are mentoring. If you have no list, then ask God to direct you to a person that you can mentor. Buy a book on mentoring to help you.

We can conclude this chapter by simply saying, unless a leader understands their ministry in at least these five areas, they will fall short of the purpose of their calling and limit church growth by being a leadership bottleneck.

Is your leadership a bottleneck to your core calling?

1 ... 2 ... 3 ... 4 ... 5 ... 6 ... 7 ... 8 ... 9 ... 10

SECTION TWO

Parading the Challenge

Chapter 5

Mission

The word 'mission' is a word that means different things to different people. The problem is that everyone sub-consciously applies his or her meaning to the word. This section of the book focuses on the ingredients of real mission. As you read this section, you will be challenged to analyse your definition of mission to see if it matches the New Testament meaning.

Purpose, vision and *mission* are words that are interpreted in various ways by different management gurus. One thing that is certain is that every leader needs these three ingredients to succeed. For the sake of my comments on mission I see *purpose* as answering the 'Why' questions, such as, 'Why do I exist' or 'Why does the church exist?' *Vision* answers the 'Where' questions like 'Where exactly are we headed?' *Mission* addresses the 'How' questions, such as, 'How are we going to get there?' Jesus understood these areas of His life very well. Jesus clearly stated His purpose when He said, *'I do not seek My own will but the will of the Father who sent Me.'*[1] His earthly vision was the redemption of the world. His mission was to live a perfect life and be the sacrifice for sin.

Purpose and vision cannot be understood in isolation from mission. The great key to our mission in life is to make sure that it works towards the fulfilment of our purpose by moving in the direction of our vision. Jesus kept Himself clean and did all that His father asked Him to do. This meant that the cross was a victory and not a defeat.

Every leader needs a mission. The whole life and ministry of Jesus *was* mission because mission is at the very heart of God the

Father. The most well-known verse in the Bible, John 3:16, is the mission statement of the Godhead. It unfolds how God the Father planned to redeem the world.

For decades the church in the West has been living in maintenance mode. Its resources and its operations have been, to a large degree, inwardly focused. It spends more money on itself than it does on mission, simply because it has not understood, purpose, vision and mission.

The emphasis of the Holy Spirit at the beginning of the twenty-first century is firmly upon mission, the 'how' of achieving God's purpose. However, our concept of how mission should be done is often limited to a twentieth century understanding. It leans on old methods of evangelism that are no longer effective. Twenty-first century mission addresses the heart, motivation and responsibility of the Christian as well as their method of delivery. It is concerned with light in the world outside the walls of church buildings. It is marketplace, workshop, and boardroom penetration. It is 24/7 Christian living. It is a demonstration and not merely a verbal communication; a lifestyle rather than a philosophy. The twenty-first century Christian is called to *be* mission as well as to *do* mission.

The thing you are prepared to die for reveals the degree of your passion and the focus of your belief. Jesus demonstrated this in His own life through the priority He gave to His Father's will and the ultimate price He finally paid in His death for mankind. The good shepherd lays down His life for the sheep.

The challenge of Christ to His disciples concerning mission can be summed up in three questions:

- Will you lay down your life for Me?
- Will you lay down your life for each other?
- Will you lay down your life for the lost?

Today across the world there are Christians who are literally doing this. There were close to 100 million martyrs in the twentieth century.[2] There have been more people martyred for their faith in Jesus Christ in the twentieth century than in all the previous nineteen combined.[3]

According to the World Evangelical Alliance, over 200 million Christians in at least sixty countries are denied fundamental human rights solely because of their faith. David B. Barrett and Todd M. Johnson estimate that approximately 167,000 Christians are presently being martyred every year. This compares to 160,000 martyrs in mid-2000 and 34,400 at the beginning of the twentieth century. If current trends continue, Barrett and Johnson estimate that by 2025 an average of 210,000 Christians will be martyred annually. (Barrett defines a martyr as someone who loses his or her life prematurely in a situation of witness as a result of human hostility.)[4] Between 200–250 million Christians throughout the world live in daily fear of secret police, vigilantes or state repression and discrimination. A further 400 million live under non-trivial restrictions on religious liberty.[5] Yet in the Western world most Christians do not even open their mouths for Christ. The Western church has to rediscover mission, but first its leaders must know a metamorphosis in this respect. The cold corridors of academic theological training put out the fire of mission within most leaders of the twentieth century. This has happened to a large degree because the lecturers are too far removed from an interface with the non-Christian, sadly leaving them, all too often, as mere theorists. They know about truth, but the truth no longer shapes their contribution, in practical terms, to the worlds of the secular and sacred. They may know the purpose and vision of the church, but there is no practical mission to the world.

Jesus emerged after His resurrection with one dominant directive: a mission to reach every man, woman and child on earth with the message of salvation.[6] That mission had a clear strategic path from Jerusalem to the ends of the world. For the remainder of this chapter I would like to suggest four characteristics that should embody our view of modern mission and if embraced, will bring our thinking into line with Jesus' approach:

1. *Passion*
2. *Purpose*
3. *People*
4. *Partnership*

1. Passion

Nobody ever did anything outstanding without passion. Professionalism alone will not melt ice, but red hot passion will.

According to the dictionary the word 'passion' can mean: 'ardent love or affection; a strong affection or enthusiasm for an object, concept, etc.' Passion, whether negatively or positively expressed, could never be defined as passive. Passion has deep feeling, deliberate action, enthusiasm, discipline, commitment, it is outgoing, communicative, compelling, driven. Does this describe your life as a leader in mission? If not, then you are part of the problem!

It is interesting that the death of Christ has become known in theological terms as His *passion*. Christ's crucifixion was the public demonstration of His driving love for mankind. His bleeding body, His aching muscles, His blistering body under the heat of the sun, His dried mouth, His collapsing physical form, plus the indescribable, tormenting spiritual pressure from the invisible world could have finished Him off and caused an aborted mission, but out of all of this trauma Christ rises in victory to proclaim to a lost world, 'I love you!' All this was summarised in these words, *'Who for the joy that was set before Him endured the cross.'*[7] Joy through pain; there is a cost that passion will pay for something better than already exists.

Paul had this same passion for souls. He said that the love of Christ 'constrained' or 'compelled' him. He was driven, propelled by an inner compulsion. He could not settle. Maintenance ministry was not in his thinking. Leaders of destiny eat, drink and think only of their mission.

We might ask ourselves, how did Paul preserve this passion? His writing unfolds to us some of the secrets. Paul lived his life out in a daily awareness of three things:

1. The second coming of Christ;
2. The fact that we must all give an account to God for our life on earth. Paul lived like Jesus with his eye on heaven and the Father's will. The more heavenly-minded we are, the more passionate and earthly good we will be.

3. Paul kept his passion alive through his belief that Jesus died
    for every person in the world. He was not prepared to keep
    God's gift of salvation a secret.[8] Paul said of himself, 'I am
    an ambassador'; he was determined to paint a different
    Kingdom picture for the world to see.

When the chips are down and the tide is going out and the
friends fade into the margins of life, passion alone will keep
the coals of mission glowing.

Passion or passive	▶ **Action plan** Are you passionate about mission, or are you just doing a job? Is mission central to your ministry or just an appendage?

2. Purpose

The word 'purpose' has sprung into our world in a new way,
mostly through the emphasis it has been given in management
training.

Purpose has a goal, it is journeying towards objectives. For
many leaders in the church, their purpose is completely wrong.
It centres on a contented church, peace in the board room, an
adequate salary, a good pension, nice people to work with, a
comfortable building, a beautiful wife, two-point-four children
etc. If you ask the members of this type of church what the
purpose of the church is, they will look at you with glazed eyes.

In 1968 I heard Dr Yonggi Cho speak in Somerset, England. He
was addressing the General Conference of Assemblies of God.
He talked about the problem he had as a young leader in getting
his priorities right. He had put God first, the church second, his
ministry third, the world fourth and his wife fifth. His wife
wanted him to go shopping with her every week, but Dr Cho was
too big and important for this. He asked God to deal with his
wife in this matter, but the tension between Chow and his wife
continued to grow, to Dr Cho's annoyance. In the end he had it
out with God. 'Why don't you deal with my wife and end this

conflict?' The answer he received from God was not to his liking. God wanted Dr Cho to change his lifestyle. The Lord said, 'You have your priorities in the wrong order. You have got the first one right, but your wife must come second, then your family, then your ministry, church and the world.' So Dr Cho had to eat humble pie and go shopping with his wife each week.

In life we can so easily pursue a purpose that is not pleasing to God. Jesus got His priorities and purpose right. He said, 'I came to seek and to save the lost. I came to do My Father's will.' The commission and strategy of Christ for His apostles was very clear: 'Jerusalem, Judah, Samaria, the world.' Their purpose was to take the message of salvation to the unregenerate. Paul's purpose and calling was to be, 'an apostle to the Gentiles'.

A purpose that concentrates on anything less than people is a failed purpose. Jesus came for people, not riches, not material gain, not power, but people.

Purpose	▶ **Action plan** Does your purpose in life engage with people? How does your purpose line up with Christ's purpose?

3. People

Our mission is people. One of the chief dangers within the leadership of the church today is that we actually move people down our agenda of priorities. For many leaders, their computer is more important than people! One person rewrote the 23rd Psalm and replaced the person of God with the computer, it makes very sober reading.

Jesus was always engaged with people. He went out of his way to meet the prostitute at Jacob's well. He moved out of His safety zone to touch the leper. Even in His parables He is concerned about people.

Purpose, vision and mission are important, but only if they affect people for the better. All management processes must become subservient to the release and maturing of the people in our churches for mission to the world, and the world is people.

People or programmes	▶ **Action plan** What is the purpose of the programme you are running at the moment in your local church in relationship to the people in your congregation?

4. Partnership

Another chord being struck by the Holy Spirit for twenty-first century leaders is that of partnership. Twenty-first century leadership needs to grasp the synergy of working together. This is illustrated in the way Jesus trained His disciples and fashioned His church. Jesus saw partnership in mission as an integral expression of church. Jesus sent His disciples out in twos.[9] There must have been a number of reasons for this, including moral support and encouragement, but also honesty. I have a strong hunch that if Peter had been alone, his report back would have sought to out-report the other disciples! We have already drawn attention to the fact that God placed His leadership gifts in a cluster of five. The early disciples understood the importance of partnership. Even on the day of Pentecost, Peter stood up with the eleven to proclaim the message of salvation.[10] It is interesting to observe that you very rarely find an early church leader operating alone. Jesus birthed the church to function in interdependance. No part of the body can say it has no need of another part.[11]

Through prayer networks, transformation videos and social action, the church is learning the importance of partnership. No local church should plan its mission exclusively. Twenty-first century leaders are inclusive. Joint ventures in mission which are trans-church and trans-denominational are the order of tomorrow's church. Spiritual death has always come to a society when the church has lost its united mission focus.

It must be stated that God seeks a united church in mission because He loves every person equally in the world. The Father heart of God in mission is neither sectarian, racial nor ageist, but embraces all who submit to the claims of Christ.

Partnership or independence?	▶ **Action plan** Who does your local church partner with to reach the community for Christ? Are you living in isolation or as an interdependent person?

The importance of a 'mission grid'

On the journey to repurposing our denomination towards 'mission church', I have used the material called *Journey into Mission Church* as a mission grid for all we do. A *mission grid* is a collection of values and principles that are integral to the function, life and ministry of a local church. The grid becomes the litmus test of authenticity with regard to mission.

Figure 1 illustrates the mission grid for the local church. On the left each department of the local church is aligned with the purposes in the centre block. They have to pass from left to right to demonstrate the outworking of these five values.

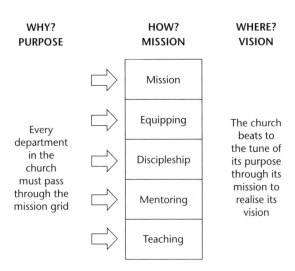

Figure 1. Mission grid for the local church

This grid disciplines the church to face the responsibility of its *purpose* (the *Why?*), its *vision* (the *Where?*) and its *mission* (the *How?*).

Every Christian leader should define a mission grid to serve their generation.

Is your leadership a bottleneck to mission?

1 ... 2 ... 3 ... 4 ... 5 ... 6 ... 7 ... 8 ... 9 ... 10

Chapter 6

Kingdom Life

The Kingdom of God is one of the greatest challenges for the twenty-first century. This chapter seeks to bring some definition to the subject, but also to stretch the leader's perception of the scope of Kingdom life and what it means to truly live by Kingdom principles.

When Jesus challenged the leaders of His day, it was very much on the issue of the Kingdom of God and what that meant in practical terms. I am sure that if Jesus were to literally walk planet earth again, His message would still be a Kingdom message, as radical today as it was two thousand years ago.

Most of us today pay lip service to the Kingdom of God, but very few of us understand or practice the Kingdom message we preach. The truth of the matter is simply that in real terms, more time and money is spent on other 'kingdoms' – material things, for instance – than on God's Kingdom. A revealing way of finding out which kingdom you are serving is to look at your bank and credit card statements to see where you spend your money.

Understanding Kingdom life

The prayer that Christ gave us to pray has this pertinent line in it, 'Your kingdom come, on earth as it is in heaven ...' God's Kingdom on earth – what does this mean and how is it seen?

The challenge of the Kingdom of God upon earth could be

likened to the rings in the Olympic flag. There are five rings, each ring representing a continent. If those rings were all separated you would have five continents operating and doing their own thing in the realm of sport, but the rings joined together show that there are governing laws that determine the actions of all athletes who want to compete in the Olympic Games.

If we look at these five rings as aspects of Kingdom life in the world, we will see the parallel, but without of course the competitive element.

- **Ring no. 1: our personal life**. Matthew 5 – 6 talks about the individual's responsibility to exhibit the Kingdom of God through their personal lifestyle. Jesus started right there with His disciples.
- **Ring no. 2: the local church**. Here is a collection of people that make a stronger Kingdom impact on the local community by means of numbers, unity, gifting and the challenge of synergy.
- **Ring no. 3: regional**. Churches working together with purpose and unity can impact bigger geographical areas with Kingdom truth, than by trying to influence the same area alone.
- **Ring no. 4: national**. Here the impact of the Kingdom is multiplied as groups of local churches join together in mission to bring God's Kingdom with a greater visibility throughout their nation.
- **Ring no. 5: global**. Leaders of denominations, networks, para-church organisations, all work together for a bigger cause than their own personal agenda to strategically impact the world for God.

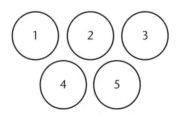

Figure 2. Rings operating independently of one another

Presently, these rings are tending to operate independently of one another, as illustrated in Figure 2, thus leaving the expression of God's Kingdom fragmented and the world confused.

The scenario illustrated by Figure 3 is what the Holy Spirit is challenging the church today to move towards.

Figure 3. The Holy Spirit's challenge to the church today

The Kingdom of God upon earth is best illustrated when these five rings join in their strategic mission endeavours to bring God's Kingdom to the world. This, I believe, is the picture that Jesus prayed to see in John 17. So, what do we learn from the Olympic rings?

Each circle on its own brings a limited Kingdom expression. It is only when the circles own each other and are prepared to surrender their own 'kingdoms' to the *real Kingdom* that the global impact that Jesus envisaged is fully realised.

People in the world view the church primarily in four different ways:

1. **Universally** – Whatever goes wrong within any section of the church is dubbed by the world as belonging to the 'universal church' in such comments as, 'So that's church is it?'
2. **Denominationally** – The more discerning look for the denominational label when passing a comment with regard to some action of the church. For example, the recent press coverage of the Roman Catholic church and the problem of paedophilia.
3. **Locally** – Within a small community the identity of a local church can emerge and take the praise or the flack for what it has done.
4. **Individually** – The life of an individual in the workplace broadcasts, for better or worse, a clear message about the nature of the Kingdom.

What is the challenge of Kingdom life for today's leader? Can we accept the principles of the Kingdom of God within our lives to the degree that they transcend our personal, local church and denominational comprehension of kingdom? Can we see the bigger picture and allow the Spirit to stretch us to understand His perspective on the church?

If we grasped the biblical mandate for Kingdom living, it would evidence itself in our leadership in a number of ways. We would naturally rejoice over what other parts of the body of Christ achieved. We would put unity higher on our agenda by uniting in joint ministries for the sake of the Kingdom. We would quantify the growth of the church beyond our local or denominational bias. We would learn from the church beyond our ecclesiastical borders.

I read an interesting article by John Smith entitled 'Change-makers – Can You Trust This Man?'[1] Smith draws attention to the way we as leaders can often be misunderstood by those who do not know the full story of what took place. He gives a great illustration of the contemporary leader Rick Warren, the US pastor behind the 'purpose driven church' concept. He quotes from an article in *The Times* magazine which had cast doubt on Rick Warren's trustworthiness. Here was the basic argument: Warren is an evangelist therefore he cannot be trusted. The journalist had done the arithmetic on Warren's book sales and made quantum leap to the conclusion that the whole thing was a money-making scheme. But the journalist did not bother to discover that when Warren realised how successful this book was about to become, he took precautions. He and his wife Kay determined not to raise their standard of living. They estimated what it would cost to support them into the future at their current level. They calculated how much Warren had received as pastor from their church in the past twenty-five years and paid it all back. They stopped drawing a salary from the church. With the remainder of the money they set up a charitable foundation to help the poor in developing countries. What a wonderful example of integrity, but also Kingdom living. Warren's Kingdom heart could see beyond his own personal life and local church to the poor in the nations of the world.

Kingdom life therefore, is not a dogma but a lifestyle. It is the expression of true Christian theology. It practises what it knows in a connectedness to the rest of Christ's body. It is more concerned about the name of Jesus than its own name, and more concerned about the impact of Christian authenticity than the success of some minor passing event. Kingdom life is about seeing the bigger picture. It is the realisation that any person, church, or organisation is only a jigsaw piece within the great picture of God's church.

Kingdom life is like the challenge of two banks. In the secular bank you invest your life, but it is not secure and yields a very poor return. Your investment is all to do with you, your security and comfort. It is restricted to a finite, earthly time zone. The other bank belongs to God and is concerned with His ideas, purposes and success. The profits are to His eternal glory. Our life and motivation can be measured by what is in the statement of the two banks.

Before Jesus sent out His disciples, He laid down the principles of Kingdom life.[2] By doing this, He made sure that what was planted by the disciples was authentic Kingdom life and not natural empire building.

The Kingdom of God or mammon?	▶ **Action plan** Take your credit card or bank statement, look at where you spend the bulk of your money and ask yourself the question, 'Who's kingdom am I investing in?'

The perspective of the church leader must always be eternity. Whenever we are about to make an important decision we need to ask ourselves, 'How does this reflect in eternity?' or 'What difference will my action and leadership directives make to eternity?' Jesus viewed life through the eternal optic. When the disciples returned from their first mission, everything had gone, except that is for the motivation of their post-ministry celebration. They were talking about their success over demonic spirits. Their celebration had all the marks of an ego trip. Jesus exposed this dangerous, intrusive enemy to Kingdom life and said these words, *'I saw Satan fall like lightning from heaven.'*[3] He saw in His disciples seeds of pride that, if not curbed, would have ruined them. Success can be a greater destructive agent than failure. On another occasion Jesus had to confront Peter, who had allowed his spiritual mind to be influenced by natural reason. The conclusion of this conflict is, in effect, his opposition to Christ's destiny as Saviour of the world. Christ's words are uncompromising and direct, *'Get behind Me Satan!'*[4] Lurking inside each one of us are opposing attitudes and actions waiting to take us away from the Kingdom life.

How powerful are those familiar words of Jesus to, *'Seek first the kingdom of God, and all these things shall be added to you.'*[5] I am asking myself continually the question about all I do and am involved in, 'What has this to do with building God's Kingdom?' Sometimes what I am involved in demands a more predominate personal role, at other times I play but a small part, whichever way it is, it must always be Kingdom. As a denominational leader this can test the reasons why you do what you do. I have a responsibility to the movement that I function out of, but that responsibility must never transcend my responsibility to serve the Kingdom of God first. As a leader, Jesus faced this challenge too. The religious leaders of His day wanted Him to conform to the traditions of Judaism, when they clearly contradicted the laws of the Kingdom. In His day it was the Sabbath, exclusivity, judgement and hypocrisy. In our day, it is materialism, denominationalism, personality syndrome, position, prosperity and so-called success.

To live a Kingdom life as a leader means we think and act in the light of what our contribution now will give to the next generation and the next life. We do not build for ourselves; we invest our lives in something bigger than any single contribution. This takes away the element of competition and releases us therefore from the stresses and strains that come from self motivation. I remember back in the early eighties being struck down with a combination of physical illnesses from septicaemia, through an embolism on my lung to kidney failure. For one week I remember very little of what happened. What I do remember however, is the incredible difference that experience made upon my life. I knew that I was now living because God had preserved my life and raised me up for a purpose. I knew then as I know today, that within a few moments, it can all be over. This is not a pessimistic statement, but a fact of life. I also knew that if that time had been the conclusion of my life, then God would have had someone else ready to take over. Isn't that a sobering fact? In the life of King Saul just two years into his reign, after his disobedience at Gilgal, his successor was already called of God.[6] Kingdom life gives you a purpose beyond the duration of your life and ministry. A good leader is a tomorrow thinker – there is no greater tomorrow than eternity.

Life and death	▶ **Action plan** Look into your life to see if there are any areas that you are holding onto for yourself. What are they and are you prepared to let them go?

Working in unity

Kingdom-minded leaders, although feeling the weight of responsibility for a section of the church, do not see their ministry or the local church in isolation from the 'universal church'. Their primary desire is to see the church grow wherever it is. They reject the competitive spirit within them. Their passion is for the Kingdom to grow and to avoid personal ambition. They do not seek to build a bigger and better church than the one down the road for an ego trip. They do not intentionally rob other churches of members. They are committed to humility because they see all members as ministers of Christ; they are building with a different value system. Paul echoes this spirit of unity when addressing the church at Corinth.[7] He calls for them to live with open hands and what a beautiful picture this is. There is no struggle or possessiveness here, only the ability to receive and give with equal delight.

The resources God has given us are to be used for God's people wherever they are. This can be a big problem to some leaders however, particularly in a growing successful church. As the church grows the leaders seem to become less Kingdom-minded and more consumed with their own local church 'kingdom'. This is illustrated by their support often, for only the ministries that come out of their church or are run by the leadership of their church. There is little investment in other ministries or community programmes that spring from other sections of the church. This happens at para-church level too. This is what has divided the church worldwide and is crippling the advancement of Christ's Kingdom in the world.

Church leadership must be a servant leadership if it is to avoid the pitfalls of previous generations. Jesus had to address this issue with His disciples even after mentoring them for three-and-half years.[8] Jesus, in His washing of His disciples' feet, did a number of things that demonstrated the Kingdom life:

- He changed position (v. 4);
- He removed the excess baggage from His life (v. 4);
- He stooped to another level, treated all His disciples equally, finished what He had started (v. 5);
- He discarded all negative personal feelings (v. 1);
- He practised the values of a different kingdom under immense personal pressure (vv. 12–17).

The authority of Christ was displayed in the supernatural expression of the Kingdom through a surrendered life, not merely the cosmetic manifestation of the super-visual.

Kingdom leaders are not ashamed of their roots, neither are they bound by them

Jesus was not ashamed of where He had come from. He declared on more than one occasion that He had come from His Father in heaven. Fortunately, His roots presented no bondage to His progress.

Denominational roots however, have unfortunately divided the church on too many occasions. The problem that we who come from a denominational background face is how to handle our roots in the context of unfolding revelation and the call of the Spirit for a united church.

There is a strange dichotomy of truth that prevails in all our lives and it is this: our roots have made us what we are, but they can also hinder us in becoming what we should be. We are not perfect and so our roots have given us both our strengths and weaknesses. When counselling couples for marriage I usually ask each partner to define their expectancy of marriage. After the initial romantic candy floss, rolling of the eyes, smiling and dream responses, they come down to earth and in most cases describe a picture not too dissimilar to their parents' marriage. Why? Because that's all they have witnessed. Their roots have set in motion ideas and values that have become their subconscious perception of marriage.

I remember wrestling for a few years with the tension of what to do with my roots – should I desert them or learn from them? One of the challenges of Kingdom life to my roots was learning how to dissect the difference between truth and tradition. My roots had both, but only the truth would set me free.

The challenge to us, the church leaders of the twenty-first century, is not only to value our roots and the roots of others, but at the same time to learn from those roots and experience 'lift off'.

God instructed Israel never to forget their roots. Roots give us life, but they don't have to determine our final shape. My brother-in-law has shaped the conifers in his garden into the outlines of animals, and they are admired by all who pass his garden. A good gardener can grow a hedge to almost any shape these days. National and local church leaders have to learn this great lesson. Once leaders realise that none of us are out to pull each other down, or to squeeze each other into a particular mould, then we can begin the learning curve; the threat is over and creative new shapes of church can emerge.

How to live out the Kingdom life in a multi-denominational world is one of the great challenges facing us in this third millennium.

Law is a box shape that may be well-defined and neat, but it has death within it. Grace has no defined shape and can therefore run where the law will not venture, as illustrated by Figure 4.

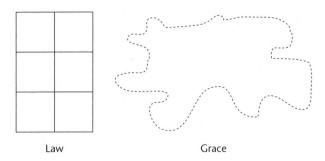

Law   Grace

Figure 4. Law and grace

Truth or tradition	▶ **Action plan** Take a piece of paper and divide it by a vertical line into two columns. Head one column with the word 'Truth' and the other with the word 'Tradition'. Now, put each part of your roots into one column only.

Kingdom lifestyle

Kingdom lifestyle simply means you live like Christ wants you to live no matter where you are or who you are with. If we look at the subject of football for instance, it does not matter where you go in the world or who you play with, everyone plays football according to the same rules. The children in the playground, the team on the pitch, and the boys in the back garden all live the 'lifestyle' of football. They follow their heroes; they try to play like the stars; they are all unashamed of who they support because they are followers of the game of football. Similarly, as leaders we must be *Kingdom people* in our thinking, our conversation, our morals and our lifestyle and play to the values of the game.

Is your leadership a bottleneck to Kingdom living?

1 ... 2 ... 3 ... 4 ... 5 ... 6 ... 7 ... 8 ... 9 ... 10

Chapter 7

Diversity in Harmony

In Ephesians 4:11 the Apostle Paul shows how teams work in local church leadership. Sadly, team ministry is missing from the bulk of church history. This chapter asks pointedly about your connectedness to other leaders. It asks about the absence of certain ministries from most local churches and asks the questions 'Why is the gift mix missing?' and 'What detrimental effect has that had on the modern church?'

I remember attending a funeral back in the seventies of a great patriarch of our denomination. The preacher on this occasion, like only a Pentecostal would do, left the pulpit and walked down to where the coffin was positioned and then turned to the congregation and said, 'Brother [naming the deceased man], was an apostle!' This comment brought a smile to my face, as it illustrated perfectly a major problem we have had historically within our group of churches – that of recognising and naming a person's gift. I knew that the dear departed brother would have never been called an apostle in life, but now that he was dead, it was quite safe to tell the truth. How strange it is that death seems to give us a freedom to say what we could not, or would not, say when the person was alive.

It is imperative that we both recognise and verbally declare each other's leadership gifts. If we have truly matured as a leader then we should be able to face the truth with humility concerning who we are, and where and how we are to function. I don't

mean we should become obsessed with title tags, but simply
acknowledge the gift God has made of each one of us.

Ephesians 4:11 immediately confronts us with at least four
obvious facts about Christian leadership. The first is designation. Designation was not a problem to God, neither was it an
embarrassment to Israel or the New Testament church. Leaders in
the Old and New Testaments were known by their name and by
their calling. If you were a *prophet, judge* or *leader* in the Old
Testament you were named as such. The New Testament follows
the same pattern. We can illustrate this by looking at the
leadership gift of *apostleship*. The following verses endorse calling,
title and name.

'These are the names of the twelve apostles . . . '
(Matthew 10:2 NIV)

'The apostles gathered to Jesus . . . '   (Mark 6:30)

*'He called His disciples to Himself; and from them He chose
twelve whom He also named apostles . . . '*   (Luke 6:13)

' . . . giving instructions through the Holy Spirit to the apostles . . . '
(Acts 1:2 NIV)

'Peter, standing up with the eleven . . . '   (Acts 2:14)

'Joses, who was also called Barnabas by the apostles . . . '
(Acts 4:36)

'The apostles and elders, with the whole church . . . '
(Acts 15:22 NIV)

*'[Paul] travelled from town to town [and] delivered the decisions
reached by the apostles and elders in Jerusalem . . . '*
(Acts 16:4 NIV)

' . . . who are of note among the apostles . . . '   (Romans 16:7)

In addition to others recognizing a person's gift, the gift holder was not afraid to say who they were and where their function was in the church. Paul introduced most of his epistles with a very clear description of who he was as the following references illustrate: 'called to be an apostle' (see Romans 1:1; 1 Corinthians 1:1; 2 Corinthians 1:1; Galatians 1:1; Ephesians 1:1; Colossians 1:1; 1 Timothy 1:1; 2 Timothy 1:1; Titus 1:1). Peter does exactly the same with two of his letters (1 Peter 1:1 and 2 Peter 1).

The character of these men qualified them to live and function in the reality of their giftings. The New Testament talks about false gifts as well as authentic ones. This implies, like all aspects of truth, that there will be counterfeit expressions of the truth that will seek to rob us of the reality of the truth. If I rejected all ten pound notes because there are some counterfeit ten pounds notes, I would be not only a fool, but a lot less wealthy! History should tell us that gift is not enough if it is not accompanied by godly character. The outstanding leaders of the New Testament were mighty because their gift was wrapped in a humility of character that embodied a pure servant heart. We must resist the 'spirit of the age' that would dissipate the importance of godly character in preference to worldly acclaim.

The acceptance of designated gifts publicly enables everyone to see that we are not all the same gift. Paul said this very thing: *'Not everyone is an apostle. Not everyone is a prophet. Not everyone is a teacher ... '*[1] Distinctives must never be confused with feelings of superiority, which are of course wrong. None of us are better or more important than anyone else in God's sight; but we are different in our callings and giftings. This diversity is important for the beauty of the church's grand mosaic of functions. Each different gift has its own special place and equipping dimension. All leadership positions are places of privilege not merit.

Another observation to make on the subject of diversity in leadership is that the Bible recognises function as being more important than rank, position or title. The disciples took three-and-a-half years to understand this one. They argued before the last supper as to who would be the greatest among them, and even after the resurrection they wanted to know about earthly position. It took a long time to get this fleshly poison out of their system and not much has changed regarding church leadership today. Unfortunately, it still peppers the church worldwide. As I travel, I realise there is a fine line between honour and elevation. We see that Paul got this balance right in his own life when he talked about apostles being the *last*, the *least* or the *worst off.*[2] And yet on the other side of the coin he can say that apostles are *first.*[3] This is not a contradiction of terms, but a clear understanding of the level at which Paul finds himself operating in different contexts. My own personal interpretation would see this 'first' position in terms of where the gift of apostle fits into the development of the church. It is clear that the apostolic gift is the first ministry engaged in the planting of a new church. The apostles, not the evangelists, were sent out to pioneer new churches. The apostolic ministry would also be the first ministry in terms of laying a foundation in a new church or relaying foundations in an old church. We can see an illustration of this both in Samaria where the apostles Peter and John were sent from Jerusalem to pray for new Christians to receive the Holy Spirit, and by definition to lay pneumatological foundations. Paul endorses this when he reminds us that apostles lay the foundation that others build upon.[4]

	▶ **Action plan**
What is(are) your gift(s)?	Write down the gift(s) you are to the church from Ephesians 4:11. It is not until you know what you are, that you discover what you need to complement your gifting(s).

Theological definitions

When we in Assemblies of God in the UK, began to wrestle with the practicality of 'going public' on gift recognition it was not easy. We had of course always believed that the five leadership gifts in Ephesians were for today. What we believed however, was not what we practised. Our two major problems were: the fear of pride and a lack of ability to clearly define the gifts. The cop-out was to call everyone a pastor. I remember spending quite some time trying to get a watertight definition for the fivefold ministry gifts.[5] I remember quite distinctly hearing God say to me, 'You will never find a definition that suits everyone.' Has it dawned on you that God is always right? I decided therefore, that all that was required for us to recognise diversity of gifts as a fellowship of churches, was to understand their functionality in a simple definition. We proceeded to do just that. The following definitions were drawn up. They are helping us to see how these gifts operate together for the mutual benefit of growth. As you will see, they are neither watertight nor exhaustive.

For the work of the apostle we said:

> *An apostle is a gift from God to the universal church whose ministry is to lay or relay foundations that others can build upon. An apostle's work precedes other gifts in function at this level.*

For the work of the prophet we said:

> *A prophet is a gift from God to the universal church that has a revelatory ministry that grounds and guides the body of Christ to fulfil God's will.*

For the work of the evangelist we said:

> *The evangelist is a gift from God to the universal church whose ministry is to proclaim the gospel, gather the harvest and inspire the body of Christ in evangelism.*

For the work of the teacher we said:

> *The teacher is a gift from God to the universal church whose ministry is to equip the body of Christ in sound biblical doctrine.*

For the work of the pastor we said:

> *The pastor is a gift from God to the universal church whose ministry is to a specific location to feed, protect and care for the body of Christ.*

You will notice that we recognise three things in these definitions. All these gifts are given to the *universal church*. That means that no local church can claim a monopoly on any one gift. Secondly, each gift has a distinctive role that the others are not equipped to bring. Thirdly, because these gifts are different, we need to be exposed to all five gifts if the church is to be truly equipped holistically.

Of course, we need to add a further two important points: firstly, we do not believe in 'Lone Ranger Ministry'. Every 'gift person' needs to be accountable to a local church. Secondly, some gifts will find a more residential role in the local church than others – the gift of a pastor is a good example of this. It needs to be stressed however, that the pastor should draw on the ministries of the other four gifts if the local church is truly going to prosper.

A local church can be likened to a healthy person. A person's requirements for health come from more than one source. One needs fruit and vegetables for vitamins and fibre, meat and fish for protein, potatoes, bread and cereals, for carbo-hydrates and water for fluid. These are the things a person requires to take in from outside of themselves. In addition to the good things they eat and drink they also need to exercise in order for the body to be toned and developed to function to its highest potential. But we also need to protect our bodies from the things that could damage or kill them. Poison and smoking will definitely reduce performance. We should avoid harmful experiences, such as standing in the middle of the London M25 at 5 p.m. on a Friday afternoon, or lying on a sun bed in 40°F temperatures without sun cream, or talking an afternoon swim in the Antarctic.

People in churches need more than pastoral vitamins if they are to grow and develop. The church needs equal input from each of these leadership gifts if it is to become a quality church. My challenge to every leader is simply this: How many gifts are the people in your church exposed to on a regular basis?

Look at what each of these gifts offers to the local church as viewed simply through these observations:

- apostolic – foundational;
- prophetic – revelatory;
- teaching – illumination;
- evangelistic – gathering;
- pastoral – protecting.

We need every gift to function if we are to see an effective church in the world.

Complete or wanting?	▶ **Action plan** How many of the five gifts are equipping your local church on a regular basis and what are they?

During the mid nineties, we were faced with an interesting situation in our home in Scunthorpe, England. We were a cell church and that meant that our home was very busy, because we had three different cells each week in our house. One was led by my daughter, another by my son and the third one by my wife and me. The problem was where to go when a cell that you didn't belong to was functioning in the house. We decided the solution lay in adding a conservatory extension to our house, so we called in a firm to build one for us. The first person to come was the architect who in conversation with me drew up the design and plans (Figure 5). A few weeks later, the brick layers

Figure 5. Artistic impression!

came to put in the foundations, lay the floor and built a low supporting wall for the windows. After they left the window men came and erected the glass and steel frame construction. They left and then the electrician came, followed by the plasterer. Finally, the job was finished. The furniture was moved in and we had our little escape room. What did we learn about this construction? It took more than one tradesman to build the conservatory and each tradesman complemented the work of the others. Finally, none of the workers had built the conservatory for themselves, but for our family.

Similarly, God designed the church to grow via a diversity of gifts working together in harmony. Whatever our job or function in the church is, we must always remember that the church does not belong to us; only Jesus can call the church, 'My church'. The church is being built for Christ our Bridegroom and for His glory alone.

I do not think for one moment that the early leaders of the New Testament church were there to feather their own nests. They were there to labour in the field of the world for the Kingdom of God.

Paul says a wonderfully illuminating thing,

> *'What the world thinks is worthless, useless and nothing at all is what God has used to destroy what the world considers important. God did all this to keep anyone from bragging to him. You are God's children. He sent Christ Jesus to save us and to make us wise, acceptable, and holy. So if you want to brag, do what the scriptures say and brag about the Lord.'*
>
> (1 Corinthians 1:28–31 CEV)

If we are to break the Leadership bottleneck we have to learn to function in our God-given gifts so that the only name on all our lips is that of Jesus.

Your church or His?	▶ **Action plan** Stay in the presence of Jesus until you have freed yourself from being possessive about your local church.

Is your leadership a bottleneck to the diversity of gifts working in harmony for the good of the local church?

1 ... 2 ... 3 ... 4 ... 5 ... 6 ... 7 ... 8 ... 9 ... 10

Chapter 8

Leader of Leaders

'Do all ministers have the same range of leadership?' The answer is clearly 'no'. The result of this is, although all true leaders are equally loved and called by God, they do not share exactly the same capacity. This means that some leaders will naturally lead other leaders. How do we discover the level of our leadership? How do we serve another leader? This chapter addresses these important questions.

I remember attending one of my first school sports days as a parent. Everything was organised well and the young children who entered the races did their best throughout the afternoon. The last item on the programme was a tug of war between the teachers and the pupils. The little children filed behind their leader on their side of the rope until there was no rope left for them to hold on to. On the other side of the rope were their opponents – the teachers. This was a serious moment in the day's proceedings. The referee instructed them to take the strain and then commanded the teams to pull. For a few seconds, the little ones held on, but slowly and surely the teachers began to win. Something happened then, that I will never forget. The parents, without being summoned, involuntarily went to the rescue of their children. Each got alongside their child and began to take the strain, eventually winning the day for their kids.

That event illustrated many wonderful things to me, such as the power of relationship, the inner call to help those weaker than ourselves or to support the underdog. It was also a picture of synergy. When that group of parents pulled together, they achieved what they could never have achieved working alone as individuals. In the twenty-first century, in all walks of life, we are discovering the power of team and the power of synergy.

Team is something more than plurality of people. It maximises the latent power within a group of people that comes to the surface only when they work together in such a way that all are satisfied. Each member of the team can experience a new level of success as a unit that they were incapable of achieving as an individual.

I remember being enthralled when listening to the experiences of Alan Chambers, the polar explorer I mentioned in an earlier chapter. I recall an incident he related from the early stages of his adventure when he was still selecting the team that would accompany him to the North Pole. After a short preparatory expedition in the Antarctic, the team returned to the station to unload. Each member of the team pulled their weight in unpacking, cleaning down the sledges and dealing with the different pieces of equipment – except one. Unfortunately, one of the team went into the station, leaving the others, and made himself a hot cup of coffee. This man was well qualified for the expedition, more so than most of the others that Alan had short listed for his team. Alan shared how the other members of his team felt about this situation and how this man's selfishness became the defining moment in his selection. Alan said to this man, 'You will not be on the expedition.' Alan could not risk having a member of the team who would prefer his own comfort above the team's success when the chips were down. Such 'team function' is a vital aspect of leadership that the modern church leader must understand.

Team was an essential part of New Testament leadership that unfortunately diminished to a large degree within the church in the third century. Towards the later part of the twentieth century in the Western world however, team leadership has been put back on the church's agenda. However, in many cases we have given recognition to *plurality* but not to *diversity of gifting*.

If the church is going to increase and expand then it must of necessity discover the true meaning of team. Here are ten reasons why leaders may have avoided working in teams:

1. It's easier to do it by myself.
2. Team leadership requires you to give up control.
3. Empowering teams reduces the perceived value of the individual leader.
4. Teams may take longer to get the job done.
5. My church hasn't done ministry that way before.
6. The church's leaders have never been trained to work that way.
7. We have not seen team leadership successfully modelled by other churches.
8. It requires clear vision.
9. It redefines the pastor's role.
10. It requires a different church culture.

Alone or team?	▶ **Action plan** From the list above tick the ones that may describe you. What are you going to do about these areas?

When I began to look in 1997 at reshaping the Assemblies of God in the UK for mission, I discovered some interesting things regarding the mix of ministry gifts among our leaders. The following breakdown is a fairly realistic description of the leaders at that time.

Pastor – teachers	64%
Pastors	10%
Teachers	15%
Evangelists	5%
Prophets	3%
Apostles	3%
	100%

I am sure that this breakdown would mirror the state of most networks and denominations throughout the world. The most striking factors that this data revealed were:

- Our denomination was in maintenance mode.
- The possibility of progress was limited because there were so few transformational gifts (apostolic and prophetic).
- The Fellowship was sound, but dying.

This meant that we had to look seriously at how we would recognise, employ and support the leadership gifts we had if we were going to halt the decay. All denominations and streams will have to address this issue sooner or later if they are to experience denominational transformation.

Looking again at the statistical breakdown of our denomination, it is important not to make the mistake of dismissing the pastoral gift simply because it signifies the largest percentage of our leadership. We need to recognise that there will always be more pastors in the body of Christ than any other gift, because people will always need caring for. The pastoral gift is not inferior to the other gifts, just different. If we are to see significant change in respect to the release of mature people into ministry however, we have to expose the body to a full complement of leadership gifting.

A closer look at the New Testament reveals the principles of both *plurality* and *diversity* working together in harmony. The following section will give a brief overview of how teams can work effectively together.

The principle of plurality

Team by its very definition must have more than one person in it. Jesus started His public ministry by gathering together a team. He called twelve men to follow Him closely and later developed another seventy disciples. Within the twelve there were different combinations of plurality at different times and for different reasons. For example, when Jesus commissioned the disciples to embark upon their first mission, the team was split up into twos. Why did Jesus do this? There could be many reasons: safety, encouragement, perhaps accountability. I have often wondered what would have happened if Peter had been sent out on his own. I think he may have returned with an exaggerated account of the new converts he'd won and the miracles that had taken place. And what about poor Thomas? He could have well become disheartened, depressed and given up! But, when we travel together with another there is an authenticity about our report, as well as support and encouragement in the mission.

At other times, such as during the transfiguration – Christ's special revelation of Himself to the team – just three disciples were present. When greater cooperation was required, as in the feeding of the five thousand, all twelve were present.

It is clear to see that Jesus did not view the leadership of the church in any other framework than that of plurality. This was confirmed by the practice of the apostles after His ascension. We see clearly that the disciples continued to travel *together*, and Paul made sure that more than one elder was appointed in every new church.[1]

All of this reflects the very nature of God who is Trinity, but it also reveals the way in which He constituted the church as an *interdependent* organism,[2] which was to be equipped by a team.[3] (It might be worth pointing out here that there is no magical number to the team.)

If we take this a little further, we can see the concept of team illustrated throughout the book of Acts. The team of disciples on the day of Pentecost was described by Luke as *standing together*.[4] This band of disciples had had to come to terms with their egos in the upper room. The day of Pentecost revealed their unity and submission to one another. On that occasion, each disciple stood behind the ministry of Peter, but all needed to be filled with the Holy Spirit.[5]

In the first missionary enterprise we see Barnabas, Paul, and John Mark functioning as a team.[6] Here we have our first picture of a church seeing and releasing resources to pioneer beyond its own boundaries. The giftings of Barnabas and Paul were obviously bigger than any local church. This was confirmed later when they were first called apostles.[7] Although these men were called and their giftings defined before they were born,[8] the recognition of those giftings came out of their mission beyond the local church at Antioch. All primary leadership gifts are given to the 'church universal', but some find their geographical application in one local church.[9]

The principle of team continues even after Barnabas and Paul separate. Neither of them journeyed or ministered alone. This of course presents to us today not only a challenge, but also a resourcing problem that the church needs to address. When some of us travel in different parts of the world where it is dangerous, or where the expectation for ministry is heavy, the wisdom of working in a team is obvious, but very often the church back home does not see the need to finance more than one person.

Team, as we have already established, can be as small as two, but it can also be as big as you need it to be. Paul had various numbers in his team at different times – from as little as four members on his first missionary journey to nine on his third missionary journey. Today, in some of the big crusades, a team will be much bigger.

On Paul's second missionary journey, team was important for continuity of task. When Paul and Silas were put in prison at Philippi, the rest of the team were still free to continue the mission. On this same missionary journey, three of the team went to Ephesus,[10] Silas and Timothy did not. The team had flexibility which added strength to its ability to cope and function. We see a similar principle employed in the Premier football league in the UK, where the squad of players is often twice or even three times the size of the team needed to play on the pitch. This flexibility is also seen in smaller clubs who often loan a player for a season from a big club. Paul's second missionary journey had this dimension too: Aquilla and Priscilla[11] joined the team when they were already on the road. Apollos also came onto the team for a short while before going off to teach in another place.[12] These insights can also be seen in Paul's third missionary journey where his team was even larger.[13]

Another important thing to observe in team is that all the members are not equal in gifting. In Paul's team, some were developing their gifts, while others were well developed – such as Paul himself and Silas. Team does not have to be permanent, changes can be made. Here are some practical reasons why team may need to change:

- enlargement of vision;
- speciality of gift required;
- availability of time; time and seasons.

The importance of team is also clearly seen in the local churches of the New Testament. Jerusalem and Antioch illustrate this well. Even though these two great mother churches occupy an important place in history, they operated in quite different ways. They both recognised diversity of team, yet manifested it uniquely.

The Jerusalem church had a team that was unique in history. Christ's twelve apostles were in one church, but were also the apostles of the Lamb. They had a senior leader in James.[14] Elders were a vital part of the team.[15] Prophets like Agabas and Silas were there, and the evangelist Philip, together with other gifts like that of Barnabas who was a prophet and an apostle.

Their emphasis in team ministry was different from Antioch. They never planted churches by design. They obviously saw themselves as the custodians of the faith for the church.[16] They carried the message of Christ first to the Gentiles.[17] They supported the church in revival in Samaria through Peter and John. They gave help to the Antioch church by sending some of their leading men Silas and Judas Barsabbas to travel with Paul and Barnabas.[18]

The Antioch mother church on the other hand, was commissioned by God to send some of its most gifted leaders to plant churches in other parts of Asia. Five of their leaders are listed as prophets or teachers. The definition of their leaders included a mix of ethnicity, those who were educated and had business acumen, and with both famous and unknown members such as Manaen and Lucius.[19] All local church leaders do not become famous, but all are nevertheless important!

In the twenty-first century we need therefore to see team as an essential part of every local church, but also as a vital part of those who itinerate. In practical terms where are you in the team stakes?

The principle of diversity

The New Testament reveals not only plurality, but also *diversity* within that plurality of team. Barnabas and Paul had different ministries. Barnabas was the prophet and Paul was the teacher while ministering in the Antioch church. Both of them however, took on a different function when they left Antioch – recorded for us by Luke at Lystra – where they were first called apostles.[20]

Diversity is an essential key to the equipping and realisation of a local church's potential. Diversity, generally speaking, will enable leaders to live peaceably together because they will not be competing for the same role. One of the confusing factors in the Western church is the designation of 'pastor' to most people in a leadership role. This is not the model of the New Testament. When Paul travelled on his second missionary journey he had in his team Silas who was a prophet, Timothy who was a pastor, and Aquilla and Priscilla who were teachers.

We know however, that disagreements can arise on other grounds apart from gifting. Paul and Barnabas unfortunately had a disagreement over the suitability of John Mark as a team member, which ultimately led to their separation. For me, the saving factor in this sad experience was that Paul and Barnabas did not try to evangelise the same geographical location. Paul and his team went back to Derbe and Lystra, leaving Cyprus for Barnabas and his team. It might be worth observing here that a team probably only needs one apostle!

Coming back to Ephesians 4:11 we see that each member of the equipping team is different: apostle, prophet, evangelist, teacher and pastor. For too many years, the pastor has been expected to equip the church in areas that he was not gifted from God to perform. This produced a 'Jack of all trades' that functioned in place of other people's giftedness, resulting in the bottleneck we experience today. During my travels as co-project director of the 'Jim Challenge' in the early nineties, I saw this leadership bottleneck so often in every section of the church. It was this bottleneck that forced me to pursue God and the New Testament scriptures for answers.

The challenge we face therefore, is to find ways in which the different gifts that God has given to His church, to equip and mobilise the people of God, can function together in harmony.

Are you an equipper?	▶ **Action plan** List the things that you are engaged in that actually equip other people for service. How much of your time in a week does that equipping task take? Do you think you are an equipper?

What can we learn from these models of team?

- Churches in the New Testament had a common doctrinal statement that each leader and church subscribed to.
- The individuals and their gifts within the early church were very diverse, yet in the economy of God for the first century church, each played an important role in strengthening and growing the whole.
- No major leader on the stage of the early church lived for themselves. There were no empire builders. Mission was their focus and Christ was their first love.

Enemies of diverse gifts working in harmony

There are always enemies to team, unity and harmony. These enemies appear locally, regionally, nationally and internationally. I am privileged to work trans-denominationally, but unfortunately, see over and over again the enemy using good leaders to stifle God's purposes for the church's progress. I remember sitting in a strategic meeting for a national united mission. The plan being put forward required each group to submit their speciality ministry for the benefit of the mission. The strongest opposing voice to the mission came from the most successful agency in the room at that time. I remember quietly asking God for an explanation for such opposition. The following words came to me: 'Success can be the greatest brake to progress.' You often find that the people who are living in success cannot tolerate what they see as competition to their place of advantage. This was of course the problem with the Jewish leaders and why they despised the popularity of Christ and His followers.

If the devil can keep us working apart, he has minimised our effectiveness at a stroke. But, what are the enemies of diverse gifts working together in harmony?

Division is at the root of all enemy attack. It's amazing how we leaders maximise the seriousness of the sin of immorality and minimise other sins. Here are three that play a part in dividing us: *pride, jealousy* and *envy*. John reminds us that pride is not from our heavenly Father's nature.[21] Pride manifests itself in one of two ways: in aloofness it says, 'Look at me I'm the best' and in its introversion it says, 'Keep away from me I don't want you to help me.' We know that pride always goes before a fall and is an attitude that isolates us from God. It is a lonely road where God's presence is a long way away. Many leaders walk a lonely road for the wrong reasons. Jealousy plays a major part in this condition. Solomon said that jealousy is as cruel as the grave.[22] It is the inability to rejoice in another person's success. Jealousy has murder within its venom. It starts with criticism, can commit murder and ends in isolation.

I am amazed how many leaders are jealous of other leaders. They cannot enjoy the success of their peers. The problem is not in those who are perceived to have succeeded, but in the heart of those whose concept of church is so small and insular that it denies the teaching of the New Testament where we all rejoice in any growth of Christ's church, wherever it is found.

Envy is that inner cancer of the soul that eats away the ministry of an individual. Joseph's brothers were prepared to put him in a pit, sell him to slavery, and take him out of the frame simply because they did not like the idea of him shining more brightly that they did. Paul's counsel was never to envy another person.[23]

In a world that propagates these very evils in its lifestyle, it would be amiss if we did not remind ourselves that these enemies must be resisted at all costs by any credible church leader today.

An opposite tactic of the enemy is to crush us by belittling who we are and what we are called to do. This brings insecurity and a lack of confidence, together with an inadequate understanding of our gift(s) and standing before God. What makes a person feel like this? It can be caused in two ways. First, by self-condemnation. People often talk themselves down and this produces a 'can't' mentality instead of a 'can' confession. Leaders must really deal with such a condition if they are going to realise their potential. This can be done by confessing the truth about who they are in Christ and what they are called to do, not forgetting, as Michelle Walker once said, 'If you think you're too small to make a difference, you've obviously never been in a room with a mosquito!'

The second cause of a lack of confidence can be the negative treatment we have received from other leaders in the past. This is where we, who are not trapped, must help by building up self-confidence in such people and acknowledging their gifts.

Isolation is another thief of good team ministry. If we are team players then we must make time to be together. It would be quite absurd if a football team never met together until they were on the pitch, and conducted their training at different grounds. Team requires good relationships to be in place. Relationship enables time to be set aside for strategic thinking, support, faith, unity and prayer, all of which enables the team to maximise its potential. There is nothing worse for team performance than the absence of team players. A modern illustration of how *not* to play as a team would be the 2004 USA Ryder Cup Team. They came to the tournament in their private jets and were reported as hardly talking to one another. They were all great individual players, but had a long way to go to learn the art of team performance.

What's your team spirit like?	▶ **Action plan** Do you see the need for team? Do you recognise any of the enemies to 'team spirit' in your life? If so, write them down and then confess them to God – if necessary putting your life right with your colleagues in the team. Are you giving enough time to the team?

The principle of leader of leaders

When emphasising the importance of team, we often overlook the issue of the leader of the team. 'A leader of leaders' is a contemporary description for an age old practice. The acceptance of such a function, in my opinion, is essential to the wellbeing and success of the church. We need therefore to establish this concept theologically for at least three reasons:

1. to resist the idea that leaders do not need to follow anyone;
2. to give grounds for leaders to lead;
3. to try and understand what sort of person a leader of leaders is.

What are the marks of a leader of leaders?

- godly;
- a tomorrow thinker;
- exceptional giftedness;
- experience;
- humility;
- followers.

Biblical evidence for 'leader of leaders'

The nature and function of God

Diversity of gift working together in harmony is first illustrated in the nature of God. God is one in three and three in one – a mystery. Here we see the perfect example of team ministry. We also see three very powerful facts:

- The unity of the Godhead
- The diversity of the Godhead
- Their individual leadership through the ages, yet the acknowledged 'leader of leaders' role of the Father. Paul sums this up in Philippians 2:10–11: even though all knees bow to Christ, the glory is the Father's.

The fact that we are unique in God's creation, being made in His own image, means there is the real possibility of us expressing His nature in the office of leadership.

Biblical examples of Old and New Testament 'leader of leaders'

God included the principle of a 'leader of leaders' when He created the structure of the angelic order by appointing chief *archangels*.[24]

Adam was the leader of his family. Abraham was the leader of a powerful extended family. Judges and prophets appeared and ministered often in isolation. Yet, running along side such expressions of leadership were others who were leaders of leaders. For example, Moses led a hierarchy of other leaders – Aaron, Hur, Joshua, the twelve tribal leaders, the seventy elders and so on. He was obviously a leader of leaders in the context of a nation. Moses chose '... *able men, such as fear God ... to be rulers of thousands ... hundreds ... fifties ... tens'*.[25] All these men were leaders who had certain godly qualities such as a *fear of God* and were trustworthy, hating dishonest gain, yet each had differing leadership levels.[26] This proves an important point, that if there are levels and degrees of giftedness in leadership, then those with lesser gifting must recognise those with greater gifting.

The picture of Israel in the wilderness and Canaan might be the nearest example we have of a church denomination, for the nation had national leadership, tribal chiefs, and later under Joshua, regional geographic locations headed up by leaders. Later on Joshua was appointed to lead his team and fulfil his destiny in bringing the children of Israel into Canaan. I don't think Canaan could have been conquered by any other form of leadership than a leader of leaders.

Many years later, Elijah appears and adds an interesting dimension to the skills of a leader of leaders. He establishes a school of prophets and commits himself to mentor his successor Elisha. Later still we have the kings who ruled other leaders, ecclesiastical leaders, militarily leaders, civic leaders and tribal leaders. It is quite clear that the Old Testament holds ample evidence of this dimension of leadership.

The New Testament cannot be understood either unless we see this principle running through it. The old religious Jewish order had a leader of leaders: *'chief priests'* amongst the priesthood.[27] Jesus establishes the church pattern of leadership by leading twelve other leaders. It is clear that Peter had a leading role among the leaders in his ministry on the day of Pentecost and with regard to his revelation that God was making the Gentiles part of the church. In respect to the local church in Jerusalem, James is the obvious leader of leaders, not forgetting that there were at least eleven other apostles in that church. The dawn of missionary enterprise in the book of Acts through apostolic leaders, highlights the principle again through Barnabas' and Paul's leadership of different teams. All these leaders of leaders were called *'leading men among the brethren'*.[28] We can add to this, the plurality of leadership in every local church in the New Testament and yet, Paul's words of instruction came for many of these churches through leaders like Titus and Timothy. The very fact that apostles had oversight of many churches reveals a leader of leaders practice was accepted, even though at times some of the people in some of the churches rebelled. We could add to this, the very epistles that were written by individuals who were leading leaders and congregations by their teaching. Finally, we see the seven churches in the book of Revelation who were addressed through their senior leader, 'the angel of the church'.

I want also to suggest that the idea that the Ephesians 4:11 gifts are given to the universal church, suggests that their function will of necessity make them in some areas, leaders of leaders.

The network argument

In addition to the precedents we find in the Old and New Testaments, there is also a strong argument for recognising 'leaders of leaders' from the best practice within the denominations, streams or networks of churches.

Leaders of groups of churches occupy 'leader of leaders' positions. Sometimes it is purely an office, but in many cases it is much more than that. People in the organisation have placed their trust in a leader to lead them. Sometimes this position has some sort of title, but that is not the real issue; the important factor is the recognition that that person has something in their leadership skills that can take other leaders to a better place in God. Sometimes we call these people apostles; at other times we only recognise their apostolic gifting in retrospect. If we require a higher level of leadership in the local church, then we must surely require a higher quality of leadership within our networks of churches if they are to grow. This of course begs the vital question, when looking to appoint or to recognise such leaders, what more do they have in gifts and character than others?

The rational argument

Christians are not mindless. We are called to serve God with all our minds as well as our strength. Whether we look within the government, the military, the education system, or the domain of professional sport, there are always those who are leaders amongst leaders. Academically, politically, managerially, in any organisation, there would be chaos without gifted people being led by other gifted people

We might therefore ask the question, why do some leaders refuse to accept this principle of practice? I can only suggest that it stems from insecurity and fears that lie beneath the surface. I can only conclude therefore, that this concern is not an argument about leadership, but rather a spiritual issue.

Leadership should be evaluated by Paul's words,

> *'Do not think of yourself more highly than you ought, but rather think of yourself with sober judgement, in accordance with the measure of faith God has given you.'* (Romans 12:3 NIV)

If the church is to stimulate growth then we cannot walk any other road than that of recognising that there are leaders of leaders. Their leadership, when willingly recognised, will focus, sharpen and expand the people of God.

What sort of leader is a leader of leaders?

We have established that the Bible provides ample evidence of the principle of leader of leaders, but what was it that characterised such people? Many, like Moses, started off with no sense of destiny for their lives. Words like, 'I am not eloquent', from Moses, and 'I am the least in my tribe' and 'I am too young', from others, flowed from the lips of these insecure men. They were not always the most talented, and they did not necessarily have the social parlance required to impact their society, naturally speaking. For example, it was said of the disciples that they were 'unlearned'. But, a leader of leaders has certain qualities that are important to this type of calling that are imparted to him from God. This often manifests itself through a divine vision given to the leader that others are drawn to follow. Nehemiah was such a leader. One old preacher once told me that the proof of your leadership is quite simple. You turn around to see if anyone is following you. A leader of leaders knows and trusts God. Even though the disciples were 'unlearned', the authorities perceived they had been with Jesus.

Modern-day leaders of leaders are often very able people who, in one sense, would probably be successful whatever profession they were in. They have the ability to see tomorrow, but also the faith and tenacity to keep going on the journey. They don't give up easily and they will make it, even if others fall by the wayside. Jesus our great example illustrates this in His own life. He knew the heights of an unswerving team loyalty, expressed most poignantly by Peter when he said, 'Even if everyone deserts you I will never desert you,' and the depths of betrayal when just a few hours later He was left to face Gethsemane and the cross alone. Dare I say that team does not always provide the entire pavement to success? Jesus quite clearly had to walk some of that road alone.

I started to be an influence for change in Assemblies of God, UK in 1984; it was not until 14 October 2004 that the movement truly recognised the role of 'leader of leaders' by giving my team and me an 84% vote of confidence to reshape the denomination by the year 2007. Those twenty years had highs and lows.

Sometimes I thought we would never make it, but something inside kept me going. Some years ago, a friend in my church gave me a piece of rock eight centimetres high by eleven centimetres long with the following words inscribed: 'The man who walks with God always gets to his destination.' Leaders of leaders don't give up easily.

Paul and Barnabas reveal the same ability to get up and start all over again when the team fails, by starting a new team and carrying on with their calling. It is this ability to get up and lead again when things go wrong that marks out a leader of leaders.

Every team needs a leader and every leader should either serve a leader or be that leader of leaders.

The challenge of what sort of leader I am.	▶ **Action plan** Prayerfully consider who you are in the team. What is your gift? Are you a follower of a leader or a leader of leaders? Settle this issue before God and your future will reflect your wisdom.

Is your leadership a bottleneck to recognising 'leaders of leaders'?

1 ... 2 ... 3 ... 4 ... 5 ... 6 ... 7 ... 8 ... 9 ... 10

SECTION THREE

Personal Learning Curve

Chapter 9

The Equipping/Empowering Factors

Is someone a leader because of his or her ability alone? What do leaders do with their knowledge and ability? Should they keep it to themselves? This chapter deals with the most common problem of Christian leaders in the Western world: their inability to pass their expertise to the next generation.

Although we have a mandate to equip and empower the saints from the book of Ephesians, for centuries leaders have only *informed* their congregations rather than *equipped* them. I have to confess that I was never taught to equip or empower people when in training at Bible College in the sixties.

Let's look at these two words for some basic meaning. *Equipping* is to do with the impartation of knowledge, skill and ability. It enables a person to have training to either do a job better, or to do something they have never done before. *Empowering* however, enables a person to be released to function in their ability using their energy and stamina to consistently accomplish meaningful goals related to their vision and mission in life.

Three keys to being an equipper

To be an equipper, understanding is required in the realm of your personal ability. This is wrapped up in the gift God has made you to the church. There is within your calling from God, divine ability to shape another person's life for Him. This is a very precious deposit from God that has been placed in all Ephesians 4:11 gifted people. An equipper also needs to realise that the equipping process cannot be done from the pulpit alone. The equipper has to engage at a personal level with the person who needs to be equipped. This calls for the leader to adopt a different style of leadership. Leaders need to come down from the pulpit and develop friendships within the congregation, spending their time sharing their expertise and willingly passing it on. The equipper sees the end product of their success as they release an equipped person into ministry and function, thus contributing to the mobilised church. Jesus was primarily an equipper, but history has concentrated to a large degree only on His teaching and His supernatural ministry.

John Maxwell[1] outlines five steps to a being successful equipper that are very helpful. The first step is one of example. Jesus started out in His ministry on His own. His ability to demonstrate became an attraction to the first disciples in the first two chapters of Mark's gospel. People will not follow you or allow you to influence their lives if they do not see a personal dimension of ministry in you that is attractive. Most leaders get stuck right here in the execution of their own personal ministry and fail to see that what God has given them is a gateway by which others can enter into ministry.

The second step that Maxwell observes is that Jesus continued to demonstrate His ministry to those disciples near at hand, showing them more clearly who He was and what the Kingdom was all about, but also inviting the penetrating questions that brought increasing insight into what it meant to be a disciple of Christ. Many writers have picked up on the point that the first part of the process of discipling others is simply for them *to be with you*. Christ became a mentor to His disciples.[2] He demonstrated before them the power of God and taught the word of God to them as well as to the crowds that followed. They learned by example how they should live, work and teach others. Equippers always have people with them. Look at your life and see how many people travel with you.

The third step is a transfer from the master/teacher to the pupil. The person you are equipping does the work and you are with them. After the disciples had travelled with Jesus for a while they were sent out by Jesus with specific instructions (Mark 6:12–13). They were now ministering to others with the help and direction of Jesus. Good equippers allow their pupils to do the work while they observe and cover them. They also allow them to make mistakes which in turn sharpens the process of learning. The equipper becomes the supporter.

The fourth step on the process is when individuals go out to do the work on their own. By the time Jesus had trained His disciples for three years, He could commission them to go out and minister on their own. Later on we see that the message of the good news spread through the multiplication of equipped people.[3] The number of disciples in Jerusalem increased rapidly and *'a large number of priests became obedient to the faith'.*[4] It should be noted that although Jesus had commissioned them to go, they never went on their own; they always travelled with someone else.

The fifth point unveils the importance of the next generation doing the same. The equipped person now equips someone else. The true test of equipping is whether those who are equipped carry on the process of equipping another generation for ministry.

In 2 Timothy 2:1–2, Paul reminds Timothy,

> *'You therefore, my son, be strong in the grace that is in Christ Jesus. And the things you have heard from me among many witnesses, commit these to faithful men who will be able to teach others also.'*

Equipping follows a cycle. We equip those who can equip others to reach the world for Christ. During most of the last century, because leaders did not equip the church, the church was left floundering incapable of equipping its new adherents.

If we are to follow Jesus' model of equipping, we must begin by selecting reliable people and take them along with us as we visit the sick, share our faith, pray, and perform other ministry tasks.

Once they've been exposed to your experience, allow them to perform the primary tasks of ministry with your assistance. And when they're ready, turn them loose empowered to repeat the process with others. It worked for Jesus; it will work for you.

When I left Bible College I was privileged to work with a great pastor named Clyde Young. He equipped me in a way the Bible College never did. He allowed me to share alternatively in the preaching and leading of the services each week. He took me with him when he visited the sick and would get me to read the Bible or pray. He also took me into the counselling room to teach me. Before we talked to the people in need, he would tell me the problem and how he purposed to resolve it. Sometimes we would come to the end of the counselling with a different solution. He would then share with me why he had changed his mind. This equipping was multiplied into every aspect of pastoral care. I had only been at the church eighteen months when Clyde was struck down with shingles that paralyzed his vocal chords. This meant that I had to become his mouth piece for the next two years. He whispered into my ear his wisdom and I performed the deeds. This was a major equipping experience in my life as a young minister. I am deeply indebted to God for allowing me to be shaped by such an equipper as Clyde Young.

Here are seven steps that may help you to begin the process of equipping:

1. Have a heart to impart what you know to others, remembering that everything you have was given you by God.
2. Make time to share what you know with someone else.
3. Be open and vulnerable.
4. Select people who are teachable.
5. Trust them with responsibility.
6. Hold them accountable for their lifestyle.
7. Be prepared to let go and release them into their ministry when they have learnt the lessons.

Your leadership experience is not for personal consumption alone, but is a window of learning for the church in general. Most leaders will only be able to mentor/equip a limited number of people at any one time. The strategic leader will choose the people that can impact others successfully and quickly.

Equipping leaders learn from the past. They have left the merry-go-round of personal promotion and they are pursuing a very deliberate policy of sharing their experiences with the present generation for an impact on the next generation.

Equipping leaders guard the present. They are not prepared to watch the present generation fall into the same pitfalls as they did, so they walk the road alongside them.

Equipping leaders see the future. They also make provision for it. They are more interested in the success of their successors than their own success. They see progress on a continual curve.

Twenty-first century church success will be measured by the degree that the body of Christ is equipped to do the work of the ministry.

The litmus test of an equipping leader	▶ **Action plan** What percentage of your congregation is functioning in the work you have equipped them for? A good equipping ministry would expect more than 60% success rate.

Keys to empowerment

Larry F. Johnston offers some helpful keys in regard to the second aspect of this chapter, that of empowerment. He gives seven keys. They are:

1. Awareness of your gift mix
2. Prayer
3. A personal Pentecost
4. Mission and vision
5. Passion
6. A willingness to fail
7. Courage

For us to be able to *empower* another person, we must know first who we are, how God has made us and why. Each one of us is unique, which is why we should never try to clone one another. We must learn from each other but never imprison ourselves in the trap of copying or cloning. It's only when we understand our personal gift mix that we can excel in bringing to Christ's body those special gifts. If God created you to run swiftly like the cheetah, run as fast as you can. If He created you to fly high like an eagle, fly as high as you can. But as an eagle, don't spend time trying to run fast! And if you're a cheetah, don't waste time trying to sprout wings![5] Quite simply, excel in what God has made you, but don't waste your time trying to be what you are not.

Each of the other six keys listed above provide the delivery of what God has made us to the ministry of empowerment. Through prayer we discover God's greatness and resource, through a personal Pentecost we experience added power for service, or as one person said referring to Peter on the day of Pentecost, 'He got his unction to function.' This in turn gave Peter his vision and mission. When you have these things burning in your heart, you cannot dispense them with anything else but passion and it is passionate people that make things happen. All of us know of course, that when we get passionate, we sometimes make mistakes. But empowerment has already factored the possibility of failure into its programme. This does not mean that we plan to fail, but it does mean that failure does not stop us going forward. Thomas Watson, the president of IBM once said, 'If you want to double your success rate, double your failure rate.' Now if you are going to live like this, then you have to have courage. Winston Churchill said, 'Success is never final; failure is never fatal. It is courage that counts.' When Peter stood up on the day of Pentecost, he had known success and failure, but it took courage to declare the message of God that day, and what a glorious outcome the church was able to celebrate.

It may be that you have experienced areas of failure that have reduced your confidence to stand up as an empowered leader. This in turn minimizes your ability to empower others through your ministry. Well, be encouraged from the words of Jesus to Peter after he had denied Jesus three times. Jesus first receives his weak but honest confession concerning his 'philo' love and then looks him in the eyes and simply says, 'Feed my sheep.' What an example of empowerment!

The test of empowered leadership	▶ **Action plan** Look at the seven points of empowered leadership and give yourself a mark out of ten for each point.

Is your leadership a bottleneck to empowerment of your local church for service?

1 ... 2 ... 3 ... 4 ... 5 ... 6 ... 7 ... 8 ... 9 ... 10

Chapter 10

The Vision Factor

Can leadership really function without vision? On paper we would argue 'no', but actually we find many local churches being led by non-visionary leaders. The local church requires more than 'maintenance ministry' (which keeps the congregation ticking over) if it is to make an impact on the communities of the world. This chapter challenges you to answer the question, 'Am I a visionary leader?'

A man phoned the police station to report that someone had stolen the steering wheel, brake pedals, gear handle, and the entire dashboard from his car. A short while later the man phoned back to say everything was now okay – he had sat in the backseat by mistake! Where you sit and what you look at determines what you see and what your priorities in life are.

Twenty-first century leadership has to face the important subject of who casts the vision for the church or organisation? The senior leader or the leader of the team should be the one to cast the vision, providing they are the right person for the position. People follow leaders not ideas. In my role as the General Superintendent of Assemblies of God in Great Britain and Ireland, I lead a team of four, each of whom are excellent leaders in their own right. One of them was explaining to a member of the NET (National Executive Team) that his loyalty was not to the denomination first, but to me as the leader. Why? Did he mean that he was disloyal to the denomination? Not at all, but he saw the future of the denomination wrapped up in the vision of a person.

The Bible illustrates this for us from Genesis to Revelation. Great leaders led people to new horizons. The leader of any team should have a much wider perspective on what God wants to do, due to their gift, revelation and experience. This does not mean however, that they know more about every subject than anyone else, but simply that they can see further and have a clearer understanding of what is needed to progress the people of God in the domain of their calling. Put simply, they were born for the driving seat. To deny them this position is to stifle their gift-flow and limit progress. To substitute them with an unqualified person is to lose the plot altogether.

Many local churches have people in senior roles who are authentic visionary leaders. But there are many more churches that have wonderful pastors with a caring ministry, who lack visionary leadership.

In 1989, Kron Ferry International reported on a survey of 1,500 senior leaders. There were 870 CEOs from twenty different countries including representatives from Japan, the United States, Western Europe and Latin America.[1] The leaders were asked to describe the key traits, talents and characteristics desired for a CEO in the year 2000. The trait most frequently mentioned was that the CEO should convey 'a strong sense of vision'. A remarkable 98% saw that trait as the most important for the year 2000. I would suggest that this requirement in senior leaders will be increasingly affirmed as we move though this new century.

The top three traits from the above report

Personal behaviour	*1989*	*2000*
Convey a strong sense of vision	75%	98%
Links compensation to performance	66%	91%
Communicates frequently with employees	59%	89%

You might ask what *vision* is. A vision is a realistic, credible, attractive future for your church. It is an ideal and unique image of the future. It is to do with *where* you are going. Larry F. Johnson defines it like this: 'A clear, compelling, magnetic and galvanizing mental picture of a desired future state.'[2] Johnson goes on to give a little cameo on each of the pertinent words in his definition. He says first, a vision must be *clear*. Paul the Apostle agreed with this when he said, *'If a bugle call isn't clear how would you know to get ready for battle?'*[3] Second, powerful visions are *compelling*. They have a driving force that thrusts people forward. Third, visions are *magnetic*. They act as a magnet that draws people forward to a preferred future. Fourth, powerful visions have a *galvanizing* effect on individuals, teams and organisations. Like a current of electricity flowing through individuals and groups, powerful visions stimulate people in significant ways, energising them and lifting them towards higher levels of aspiration and performance. Fifth, good visions are clear *mental pictures*. Although individuals may articulate the same vision using different words, each should carry in his or her mind a clear pictorial image of what the desired future looks like. Lastly, vision, unlike missions, always speaks to what the individual, church or organisation seeks to *become* or *do* in the future, often many years on.

Vision is a concrete destination, that can be finally measured in terms of having arrived, or not.

Who's leading your church?	▶ **Action plan** Look at the senior leader and ask the question, 'Is this person giving a picture of tomorrow for the people to follow?' If that leader is not, then there is a serious flaw in the church's leadership.

Characteristics of a visionary leader

Here are six key characteristics of visionary leadership:

Comprehensive vision

Within any church or organisation you will have specialists who have vision for an aspect of the work, but the senior leader has to be able to see the whole picture. I remember many years ago after an arson attack on our church building in Scunthorpe, using the calamity to rethink the use of the building. I managed to redesign the damaged area to include two extra offices. While the work was being carried out, an elderly lady came to me and said, 'You talked about two extra offices in the new development, but I can't see where they would fit.' I took the lady under the scaffolding to the place she had not been able to see before. As soon as she entered the new section and saw what she could not conceive, she cried, 'Oh now I can see it.' Team leaders can see what others cannot and they see it in the context of the whole. They see tomorrow as if it were today. This is one of the marks of identification between a good leader and the senior leader.

Biblical vision

The foundation of all Christian vision must be biblical. What I mean by this is simply that a strong vision will always have values and principles that are biblical. For example, why would we want to help people in the community? Because Jesus has called us to. His words to go into the highways and byways, and His parable on the Good Samaritan, portray the importance of reaching those who are marginalized and damaged.

If vision is not guided by biblical principle, it will eventually lead us from the path of truth. History is cluttered with leaders who had a vision void of biblical values. Vision may be specific, like housing and caring for the elderly, but it must always spring from a scriptural value or principle, i.e. to care for the widow in this example.

Vision that is manageable and achievable

Have you ever tried to construct a building using Lego bricks? Your vision is a grand one. As you build you become increasingly aware that there are not enough bricks, windows or doors to realise your dream. You either have to go out and buy more Lego parts, or modify your dream. The reason why you have run out of Lego parts is because you failed to assess, through good management, your basic resources before you started.

A team leader should not only be able to cast a vision, but should cast that vision in the light of three important factors. First, have I got the faith to believe it can happen? There is nothing worse than a vision expressed that has no faith to achieve it. This not only brings disappointment to the team, but a lack of confidence eventually in the team leader. Many visions unfortunately, are no more than the figment of the leader's imagination. But faith comes from hearing a word from the Lord, and that word will produce the faith to accomplish the deed.

Second, the leader must mobilise the resources to bring the vision about. Resources are accumulated from a number of places. There are the supernatural God-resources that faith alone can bring into being, and there are natural resources within a local church or organisation that are essential to achieving the vision, such as finance and practical expertise. During the late seventies, I embarked upon an ambitious (according to some sceptical leaders) building project. Before I signed the first contract for £195,000, I had also looked at the natural resources that were at my disposal. I knew that we had electricians, plasterers, plumbers and various degrees of carpentry skills within the church. I knew also that we had a potential measure of finance within the people that could be given to start the project. I knew too, that there were areas of expertise that were absent from our local church that we needed God's provision for. The partnership between the natural and supernatural has always been a hallmark of Christian vision. God said to Moses, 'What have you got in your hand?' His rod was known to him – he had used it in the protection of his sheep, but that rod under the power of the Almighty was to produce what Moses alone was incapable of producing.

The word 'resources' covers many areas: finance, people, premises, talents etc. To our natural resources we must add the provisions that only God can give.

The third important ingredient to achievability is perseverance. Leadership has to be able to endure when the going gets tough. Jesus is our great example here. He had a vision for the salvation of the world. Things were going well when the people acclaimed Him as king on Palm Sunday, but to realise the vision, He had to endure denial by His own disciples, Gethsemane, the cross, and the pain of loneliness expressed in the words, *'Why have You forsaken Me?'*[4] All journeys of vision have valleys as well as mountaintop experiences.

My experience tells me that even though you may have a good team standing with you, there are times when it is only you and God, and it is then that you have to believe that the wisdom and faith that God has placed within you in your role as team leader is enough to bring your through.

Inclusivity

We have established already that plurality is God's pattern of operation. In this context we discover that God has made every church unique. Paul says these words, *'God has set the members, each one of them, in the body, just as He pleased.'*[5] This word 'set' can also be translated 'arranged' (The Amplified Bible). My wife is very good at flower arranging. Sometimes I accompany her to buy the flowers. I have always been amazed at the way she selects the flowers. To my untrained eye, her selection often seems to have no logical process to it. A few hours later, when I see the beautiful flower arrangement, I understand what was in her mind during the selection process. In every local church, God has brought people together from different cultures, countries, and with different experiences and abilities. Like the flower arranger, He has gathered together a unique group of people for His glory within your local church. In fact there is no other local church in the world like the one you lead. The visionary leader has to be able to co-operate with the Master to shape and include these people in the God-arrangement for the world to see.

The New Testament includes all of God's children in fulfilling His purpose in the church. Corporate vision sees not only the many needs of the church and community, but also the potential within the people God has placed in the local church. Some leaders actually seek to discover that potential through a questionnaire that is given to all new members asking what their gifts and expertise are.

Community related

Any vision that does not step beyond the walls of the local church has failed to understand the Father heart of God.

One of the marks of a twenty-first century church will be its interface with the world outside the walls of the church building. Jesus spent most of His time on the road, not in the temple or synagogue, because He had come to reach people not buildings. The mission of the church must always be primarily to the non-Christian. As long as the church's priority is inward, its future is bleak.

The challenge of the Holy Spirit today is to prepare the people of God for 24/7 mission to the world. Every leader, and especially the visionary leader, must continually ask themselves, 'Does the vision I am propagating reach the community?' Anything less is a flawed vision.

Credible leadership

Through the years more disunity has come through competitive leadership than almost anything else. The leader of the team does not have to fight for their position. Their leadership is respected by the team because of the credibility they have in the gifting God has given to them. *Charles W.H. Scott said,* 'Leaders are ordinary persons with extraordinary determination.' If you sit with a visionary leader, you will become challenged by what he says, but there will also arise within you a desire to be a part of what he is engaged in. There is almost a magnetic pull that draws a person to the vision being presented. This of course exposes the two main characteristics of a visionary leader: he is going somewhere and he is able to persuade others to go with him.

The word 'credible' is defined in the dictionary as: 'capable of being believed, trustworthy or reliable'. It is derived from the Latin *cr dere* to believe. The Christian leaders credibility apart from his spirituality can be seen in these three areas:

1. He must know the way to go – preparation
2. He must cause others to follow – leadership
3. He must stay ahead of the crowd – perseverance

The team leader of any section of the church will have the above qualities in abundance. Our walk determines our fate.

How are you faring?	▶ **Action plan** How do you rate on a table of 1–5 on the six characteristics above?

In conclusion a good vision will be:

- *Clear* to the leadership team and congregation. It must be understood.
- *Challenging* to the people who are being asked to engage in it. We find in the secular world that the bigger the vision is, the more attractive it is to the entrepreneurial business man.
- *Pictorial* – A vision is a picture of what the church will look like when it realises its mission. It's a snapshot of what will be. A visionary leader always has the picture before them.
- *Possible* – A good vision is honey covered with potential. You can taste it because it is reachable.
- *Needful* – We don't change for change's sake. There must be good reasons for change.

Vision, mission or both?	▶ **Action plan** Does your church have a vision? Does that vision have a mission? To have one without the other will end in failure.

Is your leadership a bottleneck to vision in the local church?

1 ... 2 ... 3 ... 4 ... 5 ... 6 ... 7 ... 8 ... 9 ... 10

Chapter 11

The Facilitation Factor

Bible teaching institutions historically have had nothing to say about facilitation (the capacity to enable others to function to their full potential), yet this ability is a vital requisite in our modern society. Most leaders find facilitation very difficult to learn. See how you fare and whether or not you have this important tool in your leadership tool box.

When I attended Kenley Bible College in London, England, in the early sixties, the work of facilitation was not taught. This omission it seems has been common historically to all theological colleges in the Western world. Facilitation is a completely different leadership approach from the one most people reading this book will have been taught. In the secular world it has become a vital part of leadership practice. Jesus of course used this method on more than one occasion; the feeding of the five thousand would be a good example.

The facilitator's role

It works like this: a leader comes into a group situation to enable that group to realise their potential, clarify their strengths and weaknesses, assist that group to define its purpose, objectives and strategy, and to help them work together as a team to achieve them.

I remember the difficulties I faced in learning this aspect of leadership during the early stages of introducing a cell structure to our church in Scunthorpe. Over and over again I talked too much, or imposed my ideas on the group, or failed to listen; not to mention the missed opportunities of developing the ideas and gifts of those in the group who would make the vision happen. As time went on my team lovingly corrected me by saying things like, 'Be quiet and listen or you will be *teaching* us not *facilitating*.' At the end of each session I would be appraised kindly on my performance as a facilitator. I must admit it was a big learning curve for me, but has aided my leadership skills in a profound way today. So, what does a facilitator seek to do? There are four facets I would like to highlight:

Seek ownership by consent

The twentieth century leader imposed his/her vision on their congregation. But, the facilitator seeks ownership of the vision by presenting the *challenge* rather than the *solution*. As people contribute, they increasingly take ownership of a shared vision. It should be pointed out however, that although this is now an accepted way of realising the potential of people in general, it works best with those who have more ability. A leader therefore, might choose to use this method particularly with their leadership team.

Ownership is a priceless ingredient in all successful teams. 'Consensus-ship' is an important part of arriving at ownership, but should never be confused with compromise or democracy. A good facilitator will not allow the group to duck the difficult issues, but rather will face these because they know that true ownership will only come when all matters in the equation are confronted and solved to form the foundation for the next stage of the journey. Now I know that some of the leaders reading this book will be saying, 'But hold on, I have been called to lead and does this not compromise my leadership calling?' Good leadership cannot be compartmentalised into one area. A good leader, like a good craftsmen has many tools in their workbag. There are times when leadership has to say, 'This is the way – let's go.' There are other times when the objective is clear, but the process is not.

Make space for others to contribute

The Bible talks about wisdom being in the council of many and makes the point that iron sharpens iron. Twentieth century leadership very rarely made space for the contribution of others. Church leaders got away with this because to a large extent they were ministering to loyal people, who had been educated to follow and know their place. This loyalty factor was very much a part of pre-sixties Western society and reflected the culture of the day. Today children are educated differently. Rather than being taught from the front of the class, they sit in small groups, they research their subject, and they are trained to ask questions, challenge concepts, be participatory and so discover truth, rather than be dogmatically informed of it. We can no longer rely upon the luxuries of loyalty and allegiance from society; therefore leaders omit the consultation process at their peril.

Draws on the expertise of others

A facilitator sees in any group, experience, expertise and potential that is diverse, but that can become powerful and effective if harnessed. The day of one person having all the expertise has long gone. Some years ago I sat in a graduation ceremony where the chancellor of the university said something that made me think: 'We are not training our students for one profession in a life time, but for seven or eight changes of profession in a life time.' What does this mean? Simply this: the people we are leading in our churches have the ability for change; their education has equipped them to be adaptable and to contribute in a multitude of different ways. They are not plumbers, or bankers, or engineers alone, they have the capacity to switch professions. Built into their education is *flexibility*, which means, in the context of a group being facilitated for a project, there are people who can change their role to serve the new cause.

Empowers others to function

I remember many years ago having my eyes opened, under the old system of church leadership operation, as to why some people seem to have most of the work. A friend said to me that, 'The one who walks out of the room with the most paperwork is the one that the heaviest workload falls upon.' The amazing truth is that the most paperwork has landed historically in the lap of the church leader. The rationale of congregations, elders and deacons was, 'That's what we pay the minister to do.' The results would have been laughable if they had not been so serious! Leaders tried to do what they were not trained to do, and some fell by the wayside in physical, mental, and domestic breakdowns whilst the congregation largely remained spectators waiting for the next leader to take up office. Leaders have injured themselves by not learning the art of facilitation. A facilitator is not expecting to leave the room with all the paperwork destined for their desk, quite the reverse. The facilitator is there to facilitate the function of others. It is an empowering leadership. Every member of the group should go away with a personal portfolio that has expectation, responsibility and accountability built into it for every stage of the journey.

The facilitator's attitude

A facilitator does not come with all the answers. Their role is not to tell the group what to do, but to provoke participation in the group. The hardest thing for a facilitator to do is to keep quiet and wait for the group to provide the answers. A facilitator must have a clear understanding as to what they want to achieve from the session with the group, but also a teachable spirit that allows them to make a better contribution. They also need to have a sense of fairness in the discussion process, so all feel they have played an important part in the exercise. There are three keys to the facilitator's attitude that I want to highlight:

They lead but do not enforce
Their job is not to provide verbal answers, but rather to lead the group to a self-discovery of the answers through the talents and gifts within the group or through expertise that they can harness from elsewhere. They act as a link from one section of thought to the next. They use open ended phrases like, 'So how could this work,' or 'Why can't we do this,' or 'What does this mean?'

They know where they are going, but they don't let on

A good facilitator knows where they are going in order to achieve the purpose, but they act as if they have no answers. This does not mean that the final outcome will be exactly as they intended it to be, quite the contrary; they know that the group will make the final solution better than they as a facilitator originally saw it. For example, if the facilitator's job was to produce better door stewards for the church, they might see that there is need for extra stewards, better dressed ones and for them to be more competent. The group however, might accept the challenge of more and better stewards, but suggest there should also be male and female together with a cross-section of age groups. They might also suggest that training would be necessary and that the training should reflect the purpose of the church. They might also offer to train and supervise those new stewards and to evaluate their performance every six months. Perhaps they would suggest that there ought to be thought given to the next generation of stewards and perhaps a second group of stewards who could alternate on a monthly basis to allow the other stewards to enjoy the services etc.

The original intent of the facilitator has not been discarded, but enhanced by the contribution the facilitator has stimulated from the group. Everyone comes away from the exercise feeling they have not only contributed, but have taken ownership of what they have decided. All this is achieved by the facilitator asking open and pertinent questions that feed discussion and challenge the status quo.

They are able to assess people's abilities by observation, contribution and attitude

All the time the facilitator is watching the body language of the group, listening to the contributions, observing who the leaders are, and making mental notes on those who are innovators, creative etc. The attitude of the facilitator should be a sense of satisfaction only when the group have achieved their purpose with as little contribution from the facilitator as possible.

The genius of facilitation leadership is the creativity of the facilitator to see what needs to be done and to extract from the participants the necessary engagement and solutions for the needs to be met in the most interesting and exciting ways.

The facilitator's goal

The facilitator's goal is to bring the meeting to a conclusion knowing that the following six objectives have been met:

Knowledge of what they are expected to achieve

A good facilitator will summarise what the group have already discussed and decided. They will be able to map out how the discussion and conclusions are going to be enacted into reality.

Group ability

The facilitation process is an excellent process for 'people discovery'. There are many exercises you can use in order to find out what each person can do and how their personality can be maximised within the group.

Group contribution

The group members need to know their roles, and be affirmed in them by the group and by the facilitator.

Group ownership

Because the group have worked through challenges in the light of their collective abilities, they have also come to *own* the project. The project has not been imposed upon them, but it has been taken on from conviction through to process.

Group accountability

Each member of the group must know not only their role, but who they are accountable to (line manager) and who they can consult with if in difficulty.

Group responsibility

Each group member must know the deadline for their contribution to be completed, how it fits into the work of other team members, and when the next team meeting is.

The group are now fired with enthusiasm but also know the timescale for their contribution and that of the whole project. The beauty of the facilitator's role is this: the blame for any error does not come back to the leader, but is absorbed by the group.

How are your facilitating skills?	▶ **Action plan** Does this type of leadership frighten you? Are you prepared to learn this skill? How are you going to develop this aspect of leadership?

Is your leadership a bottleneck to the facilitation of other people's viewpoints and ministries?

1 ... 2 ... 3 ... 4 ... 5 ... 6 ... 7 ... 8 ... 9 ... 10

Chapter 12

The Entrepreneurial Leader

This section faces a subject that has hardly been discussed in teaching about Christian leadership. Although it is not talked about, it is practised in most successful churches. What do we mean by 'entrepreneurial leadership' and are you an entrepreneurial leader?

My observations of successful church leaders have led me to appreciate a quality in many that we could call *entrepreneurship*. I realise of course that the very use of this word in the context of evangelical leadership could easily be misunderstood. Nevertheless I feel it encapsulates a very interesting dimension of twenty-first century leadership.

The word 'entrepreneur' means: *the owner or manager of a business enterprise who, by risk and initiative, attempts to make profit.*

The part of this definition that is important to this chapter is the middle part; *'by risk and initiative'*. Here are described two very important parts of a leader's role. When translated into spiritual language and context, they can be termed *faith* and *action*. Let's consider how this works in practice.

Entrepreneurial leadership sees opportunity

Jesus shows us in the parable of the talents that what the people do with their talents is determined by the factors of faith and action.[1]

The five talent person invested his money and returned ten talents. The three talent person also invested and made five talents, whereas the one talent person showed no faith or positive action and therefore no return. The end result was that the person who generated ten talents received the highest commendation and an extra talent; the person who generated five talents is also commended. Both these were entrepreneurial. The non-entrepreneurial person lost out with both a reprimand and the loss of his talent.

I have many memories that reflect the difference my entrepreneurial gifting made to an otherwise impossible task. My own house has been used as collateral three times. My supporting wife had to believe that what I could see was truly of God or we would be out on the streets! An entrepreneurial person not only sees the opportunity, but how to capitalise on that opportunity. Jesus said in another place that the people of this world are wiser than the people of God.[2]

The Bible records many examples of entrepreneurial leaders. To the young fearful prophet Jeremiah, the challenge of God was to see more than he had previously seen, *'What do you see?'*[3] To Moses it was, *'What is that in your hand?'*[4] In the case of Abraham and Lot – Abraham saw the promises of God, Lot saw only the lush grass.[5]

Twenty-first century leadership requires leaders who can think and see outside the box. They need to be able to see the potential within the church, the resources of the Almighty, and the transformation that is possible within the congregation and the local community. It takes a certain kind of person to see through the darkness and believe for light.

What do you see?	► **Action plan** Does the entrepreneurial dimension come easily to you, or is it missing from your ministry? If it is missing, then you need to seriously think about where you are going to get the input for this important gift within your leadership.

Entrepreneurial leadership seizes opportunities

It's one thing to *see*, but another thing to *seize* an opportunity. A few years ago I was on holiday in Turkey. One day, my wife and I were in an outdoor market. As we walked around the stalls I was intrigued by a man who was buying excessive amounts of merchandise, dozens of socks, shirts and other items. Finally, my curiosity got the better of me and I sidled up to the man and said, 'Why are you buying so many items of clothing?' He smiled back and said, 'Oh I do this every year. We come with empty cases and buy enough clothes to sell in car boot sales back in the UK. This pays for our holiday each year.' My wife had to hold me back because I was into the idea of a free holiday. That's an entrepreneurial man who seized the opportunity of the day.

The biblical story of the twelve spies who went to investigate the Promised Land is the story of opportunity. Ten spies saw the land of promise flowing with milk and honey, they even brought the grapes of plenty back, but the many negatives aspects about possessing the land that they saw stopped them seizing the opportunity. Thank God there were two spies who saw the opportunity of taking the land and were ready to possess it. Joshua and Caleb, these great men of faith and action, were eventually to realise their dream.

Every day opportunities are given to us by God that, if taken, will bring transformation. Perhaps you can look back and see opportunities that you have missed. The devil wants to use these to demoralise you and reduce your effectiveness. The best way to deal with these negatives is to learn from what you did wrong, brush yourself down, ask God to forgive you, and open your eyes to the next opportunity, seizing it with both hands.

The book of Hebrews chapter 11 is filled with those who saw and then seized their opportunity. Faith is an action. It is better to have tried and lost than never tried at all. In 1993 my friend Phil Weaver (no relation) and I were faced with a national challenge to win 200,000 people to Christ in one month. The goal was ridiculous, but we prayed and the Holy Spirit lifted our spirits to believe for an impact on our nation. The Jim (Jesus in Me) Challenge was born and inside eighteen months we raised

£2.5 million in cash and kind. Many of the ways in which we raised the money were entrepreneurial. We saw thousands of souls make decisions for Christ, placed an outreach magazine in every home in Great Britain, made the first Christian advert for national television, produced materials for new converts together with 'know how' material for witnessing, and so I could go on. We seized the opportunity.

Since the eighties I have been working on denominational reformation, because I have come to see a better way of doing church than we have been engaged in historically. I am still on that journey; some have lost sight of the goal, others have lost stamina for the journey, but the entrepreneurial leader inside of me keeps going.

Entrepreneurial leadership thinks laterally

'Lateral thinking' is a phrase that describes a way of thinking that is different from normal comprehension. Collins Dictionary defines it as, 'a way of solving problems by rejecting traditional methods and employing unorthodox and apparently illogical means' (an example is illustrated in Figure 6).

The Kingdom of God is built on lateral thinking. It functions in opposition to almost every human thought process. Perhaps that's why we can only understand it by faith! Here are some

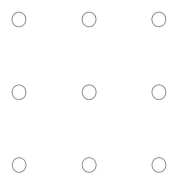

Figure 6. A lateral puzzle. The test is to pass through all nine dots by drawing four straight lines without taking your pen off the paper. (The answer is on p. 128.)

examples: you die in order to live; you give away in order to receive; you love your enemy; you turn the other check when opposed; you rejoice when persecuted and you forgive when transgressed against.

Not only does the gospel challenge our thinking, but the lifestyle of Christ which was quite unorthodox also challenges our practices. Jesus healed people on the Sabbath; He had women travelling with Him; He talked to publicans and sinners; He sought no personal material gain for His ministry (that would be a difficult one for many Christian leaders today); He found supernatural solutions for earthly challenges; and the feeding of the five thousand just blows our minds. Jesus was not stuck in a box! He lived as a man inspired from eternity. On earth His thoughts and ways were alive and unpredictable, yet coated with immense wisdom and insights that shattered the concrete minds of those detached from the Creator God.

The twenty-first century leader will not be able to impact a post-modern era with conventional thought processes. The post-modern challenge requires the unpredictable, but not the irrational. All of Christ's actions were based on clear operational principles. Jesus moved by value and principle and so was able to operate beyond the conventional.

I remember growing up in a good local church where people loved me and cared for me, but nevertheless many of those same people were entrapped in traditional ruts of restriction and would have found it almost impossible to respond to anyone who thought or acted outside of 'the box' of their way of doing things. I thank God that today increasingly, the church is facing the opportunities that godly, lateral-thinking leaders are providing.

Entrepreneurial leadership has a big God

The Christian entrepreneurial leader perceives ways uncommon to that of tradition because they see the ways of God. We often comment that God's ways are different from ours, and even rejoice and stand in amazement when those different ways are recorded in the Bible, yet we are often the first to criticise God's 'different ways' for the church today!

I was greatly challenged in Berlin by the ministry of Sunday Adelijah, a fine young leader who planted hundreds of churches during the nineties. He put the secret to his success down to a monthly week of prayer that he has with God alone. Each month he hides himself away from the church, his family, the telephone, and any other distraction and seeks the mind and heart of God. He says, 'I seek to do three things during this time. The first is to bring my life to the place where I totally believe that only God can do it. The second is to enquire of God regarding how He is going to do it. The third is to commit myself to doing it God's way.' Sunday then returns to his church and ministry to do God's will by faith.

Faith can only truly act when it is directed and connected to the eternal God. The greatness of God travels through the spirit, mind and heart of the Christian to lift them to a plain of insight, faith and vigour that cannot be manufactured outside of such a God-encounter. Those who dwell on the greatness of God grow in faith and accomplish great things.

Amy McPherson always preached a **BIG GOD**. Paul the apostle was a man with a big God: *'Who can separate us from the love of God?'*; *'If God is for us, who can be against us?'*; *'I can do all things through Christ who strengthens me ...'*[6]

It should be noted that entrepreneurial leaders do not *make* God 'big', they simply allow their leadership to be affected and expanded by the greatness of the God they serve.

Entrepreneurial leadership is unconventional but trend setting

Biblical and church history reveals the fact that all entrepreneurial leaders who operate under the direction of God become the 'trend setters' for the next generation. They open unseen doors for others to walk through. Moses and his 'Red Sea experience' paved the way for Joshua to go through the Jordan. Caleb fighting the giants in the Promised Land became an inspiration for David to kill Goliath. Jesus walking on water was the inspiration for Peter to walk on water. There are many men of inspiration and entrepreneurial prowess who have broken through barriers for the church to follow: Rick Warren and the 'purpose driven church' concept, David Yonggi Cho and cell church, Caesar Castellanas and the G12 model of cell, Bill Hybels and the seeker-friendly church concept, Sandy Miller and Nicky Gumbel and the Alpha course. All these were unconventional at their inception, but are setting the trends for new and relevant church today. God has not called us to copy one another, but to go to the source of revelation ourselves to find God's way of reaching mankind for Him.

The subject of entrepreneurial leadership is not addressed in this book to give licence to irresponsible leadership action, or to argue that all unconventional leadership will lead to success, but is addressed to show that God can make a leader see new ways of leading the church to impact the world that are not necessarily traditional. Paul prays in Ephesians 2 for a great invasion of the illuminating power of the Holy Spirit to break in on our hearts and minds. This prayer is for a revelation of what the church *is* and *should be* in the world today. Any leader who sees this will find an application of function to the society in which he lives that can be described as entrepreneurial.

Is your leadership a bottleneck to entrepreneurial contribution?

1 ... 2 ... 3 ... 4 ... 5 ... 6 ... 7 ... 8 ... 9 ... 10

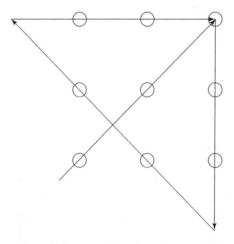

Figure 7. Answer to lateral puzzle on p. 125

Chapter 13

The Management Factor

Management and leadership are two different areas of operation, yet all leaders must have an understanding of management. What is management and where does it fit among the varied tasks of ministry? This chapter highlights the importance of different aspects of management and its relationship to leadership.

Some leaders manage by instinct rather than by education. Some of us have read a few books, learned a few lessons, and sat in a few seminars on the subject of management, but to a large degree have shied away from full frontal collision with this important subject. There are many reasons for this. One is that historically, management and Christian leadership have been seen by some as enemies. In many evangelical circles the idea that our interaction with God could be 'managed' was incomprehensible. We are gradually discovering however, that the management of the church is nothing to do with us 'managing God', but of God using us to manage His work in His way.

I am not qualified to handle such a large subject as management in a book, let alone a chapter. My purpose in inserting this chapter is simply to highlight the importance of this ministry in the church today. The need for expertise in managing people for God is at the very heart of biblical understanding. From Adam and his role in the Garden of Eden, through to the Temple structure in the Old Testament, to the running of church in the New Testament, we see management systems in place.

Management could be defined as the technique, practice, or science of controlling the skills, resources of people, materials and time for profitable ends. If equipping and releasing God's people for ministry is a part of the modern leader's function, then the management of those equipped people is also a vital part of the leader's armoury. Jesus understood this and we see His expertise in practice when He fed the five thousand: He had them sit down in groups of fifty; He used His disciples to carry out the distribution of bread and also used the same management system to leave the field clean afterwards in an eco-friendly act. None of His managerial skills conflicted with His reliance on the supernatural power of the Spirit to perform miracles, quite the contrary – the management aided the dispensing of the miracle bread in order for everyone to be filled.

In November 2003, I employed a management consultant to help me with the reorganisation of the Fellowship of Assemblies of God in Great Britain and Ireland. For some, this seemed an unnecessary thing to do; we have survived for eighty years without such help, so why did we need this influence now? But within one month, the insights of this man further underlined to me the importance of good management skills. I could see that whatever we had achieved in time past could have been multiplied if we had had good management in place.

As I visit local churches I see all too often a lack of good management in the church. Sometimes the good ministry that is delivered on Sunday is lost to the world by Monday, simply because there was no extension of that delivered message through good marketing and lifestyle to a wider area of influence.

In chapter 10 we looked at *vision*. It is true that nothing happens until there is a vision. It should however be strongly observed, that a vision will not happen without the underlying practicalities of purpose and the support systems of good management.

Here are three areas of management to consider:

1. Management and mission;
2. Management and leadership;
3. Management and values.

Management and mission

History illustrates that many Christian organisations started out well but lost their identity because of an inability to keep their organisation fulfilling its purpose. This was one of the challenges that I faced in looking at the purpose of Assemblies of God in the twenty-first century. At its inception in 1924 it was clear that there were probably three main reasons for it coming into being. The first and most significant was to spread the message of the importance of the baptism of the Holy Spirit. The second was to form a movement for fellowship and identity for those leaders and churches who believed in this experience of the baptism of the Holy Spirit. The third was to take the message of the gospel to the world in the power of the Holy Spirit. As the years have gone by, the need for the first area of purpose has diminished because of the church's acceptance, to a large degree, of the baptism of the Holy Spirit. Today, the Pentecostal sector of the global church is the largest. The need for fellowship however, still exists even though relationship is increasingly trans-denominational. The final reason is a timeless reason that should be owned by the church universal. So, where do we stand today in terms of our mission and what sort of management is required to sustain our purpose in this third millennium?

In the light of what I have just explained and in order to address the 'Why' of our existence today, I had to redefine our purpose for being. In 1996 we wrote a statement summarising our purpose for being which read, 'The purpose of Assemblies of God is to give every man, woman and child the opportunity of understanding the Gospel and to provide a church where they can grow and develop in ministry for the glory of God.' This purpose reflected not only our mission but also the importance of the mission of the church in the world. I remember one of our leaders angrily commenting when I had first announced the new purpose, 'Where's the Holy Spirit in this purpose?' He had seen the absence of the words 'Holy Spirit' as signifying my denial of the importance of the work of the Holy Spirit. My answer was simple: we must carry out this purpose in the power of the Holy Spirit.

Management however, needs visionary leadership. Colin Powell defined leadership like this: 'Leadership is the art of accomplishing more than the science of management says is possible.'[1]

It's one thing to state all this, but how do we implement it? Through a clear management process that delivers the objectives that we have set out to achieve. For us this meant a rediscovery of the role of leadership in our Fellowship and new core capabilities to resource our purpose. All this meant restructure and reformation.

I remember facing a similar situation in the local church I pastored in Scunthorpe, when we moved from democracy to theocracy. The church at that time had no stated purpose. Its major decisions were made at church meetings. When I saw that democracy was not the practice of the New Testament, I had to look at how a church might function in leadership and managerial terms outside of such a democratic system. I studied the New Testament for clues of operation and gradually saw a different kind of church management that required a paradigm change in the thinking and practice of our church. New management was required for a new operation of structure.

Is your mission managed?	▶ **Action plan** Look at the mission programme of your church. Is it purely inspirational, or does it have some management structure and process to it?

Management and leadership

Management is to do with *people* and *process* and therefore it is to do with other leaders too. In chapter 8 we spent some time looking at the importance of 'leaders of leaders' from the Ephesians 4:11 passage of Scripture. This same passage highlights the importance of equipping people in the process of 'reality church'. This in turn introduces the need for leaders with other areas of expertise than those contained in Ephesians 4:11. Paul the apostle addresses this need in some of his other epistles.[2] These other leaders fit into the process of the management of the church. The question is *how* do they all fit together? (See Figure 8.)

Figure 8. Church management and leadership

Administration – *the management of* details

The concept of administration is based upon the Greek verb *diakoneo*, meaning 'to serve'. Administration could be viewed as an 'add on' ministry – *ad-minister*, another type of ministry. The apostles in the Jerusalem church were very keen to use this ministry when presented with work that was not in their remit to execute, namely the daily distribution of food for the widows. Their specific calling was to prayer and the word of God.[3]

Management – *the management of* people

The Greek verb *proistemi* gives us our meaning for management, meaning 'to stand before, to set over, to preside, to rule, to govern'. We find in the New Testament that the elders and the pastoral gift very often fulfilled this aspect of leadership.[4]

Organisation – *the management of* structure

The word behind organisation is the Greek word *kubernesis*, which means to 'steer, guide or pilot'.[5] If we think of a ship at sea and the work of the pilot guiding that ship in the right direction, we see a very different role from that of the administrator which is taken up with the detail of the journey, or those who are overseeing the crew and cargo. The pilot waits only for the instruction of the captain; he cannot get involved in other things if the ship is to arrive safely at its destination. Organisation manages structure.

Organisers think in terms of milestones, concepts and strategies. This is often referred to as 'operational management'.

Vision – the management of the future

Visionary leadership springs from the Greek verb *hegeomai*, which primarily means 'to go before and guide; to lead'.[6] Vision, if it is to be successful, must not only see the future, but be able to see how the future can be managed. This is often called 'strategic management'. Here, the primary leader(s) have the responsibilities of seeing what needs to be done, planning how that might be achieved, and keeping everyone aligned to that vision.

Without that clear leadership gift, the people are left in a cul-de-sac or led down a road that they have no managerial control over. The key to understanding organisation is that these four areas are essential to the success of each individual part. In other words the greatest visionaries in the world will not succeed unless they have the backup force of the other three areas.

What is the composition of your leadership?	► **Action plan** Are you overloaded with one type of leader? Analyse where your strengths and weaknesses are and seek gradually to balance out your team to provide a cohesive management of your affairs.

Management and values

Increasingly, the secular world is realising that values are important to vision and mission. Quigley states, 'Values and beliefs are the most fundamental of the three elements of vision ... values precede mission and goals in logic and reality. Consequently, primacy in the corporate vision is shifting from corporate mission to corporate values.'[7] This statement completely harmonises with the execution of vision and mission illustrated in the ministry of Jesus. He introduced the Kingdom of God with two powerful foundational bricks, namely Word and Spirit. He demonstrated the supernatural with signs and wonders, but through clear words of teaching, laid down the values of the

Kingdom.[8] In fact, the disciples were not allowed to lead until they had learned the values.

I have increasingly learned the importance of value-based vision. I would die for values but never for a model. Value-based vision enables you to exercise your leadership outside of personality preference. It is not only right, but advantageous in so many different ways. For example, it enables you to exercise your leadership outside of personality preference. That means you can honestly deal with any person based upon the higher law of the values you live by. Jesus was more mindful of the values of the Kingdom than He was of upsetting people. What are the values of your vision?

It is not helpful to have too many, most people say between five and seven.

Is your vision value based?	▶ Action plan
	A vision without values is a passing vision. Examine carefully your vision and underpin it with sound values.

Is your leadership a bottleneck to good management?

1 ... 2 ... 3 ... 4 ... 5 ... 6 ... 7 ... 8 ... 9 ... 10

Chapter 14

The Responsibility/Accountability Factors

Are you a dictator? Are you doing the work you were called to do? Who are you and who are you accountable to? These questions and more are faced in this chapter. To lead without knowing the answer to these questions is to execute a very vulnerable leadership.

To be a leader in the Christian church of the twenty-first century is probably one of the most exacting jobs in the world. Central to every leader's gift must be the twin factors of *responsibility* and *accountability*.

The leader's responsibility

Historically, the responsibilities of a leader were mainly viewed through the pastoral window. Many of these duties however, should never have been carried out by the leader. Here are five responsibilities that cannot be delegated:

1. The responsibility of personal intimacy with God

As a light bulb depends completely on electricity for its energy source, so Christian leaders have no light, power, revelation, or lasting influence outside of their daily dependence on God. God designed the church so that it could only function properly when it runs on the life of God (the theme of the Ephesians epistle). There is no substitute for prayer; it is the Christian's vital breath. This is the area that the enemy will constantly seek to demolish. A leader out of touch with God is merely a human being. A prayerless leader is someone who seeks to drive a car without an engine, or to play a ball game without a ball, or to write a book when illiterate. Intimacy with God is something that only leaders themselves can develop; no person can do it for you. It boils down to you and God, or you without God. What is intimacy with God?

Time spent with God

You can spend time with a person in many different ways. You can say that you have 'been with' a person, when really you have never talked to them or shared anything of significance with them – you were simply in the same room, physically.

Time spent with God must involve two-way communication and it must be a meaningful time. To come from the presence of God having listened, shared and reflected will always sharpen the meaningfulness of our life and ministry to others. It has to be seen as a top priority for your life. God is the most important person in each day of our lives. Daniel prayed three times a day. He disciplined himself morning, noon and night to have quality time with the Almighty. He was not prepared to sacrifice that time even when his life was threatened.

Aristotle said, 'We are what we repeatedly do.' Our character, basically, is a composite of our habits. 'Sow a thought, reap an action; sow an action, reap a habit; sow a habit, reap a character; sow a character, reap a destiny', so the maxim goes.

Horace Mann, the great educator, once said, 'Habits are like a cable. We weave a strand of it every day and soon it cannot be broken.' Well, as Christians we know that habits can be broken, but not always easily.

Create a good habit of intimacy with God. It has been said that if we do something for forty-one successive days, we will form a habit. Intimacy with God is a necessity, so create quality time with God by forming a habit of prayer.

An ear attuned to God's voice

Young Samuel did not know how to distinguish the difference between the voice of God and the voice of man. Like every other voice we learn to recognise in life we have to acquire knowledge of the sound of the Master's voice. Eli counselled Samuel to say, on recognition of that voice, *'Speak, for your servant hears.'*[1] For the rest of Samuel's prophetic life, he was guided by the voice he came to know as a child.

Christian leadership is faced with a multitude of voices beckoning for a response. Each voice may be valid, but one voice must be supreme. The prophet in the Old Testament had to learn on one occasion that God was not in the wind or the fire, but in the still small voice.[2]

An obedient heart

Twenty-first century leaders will have to increasingly learn the importance of being obedient to what they hear God say. Peter had to learn this lesson when he was called of God to share the gospel with the Gentiles in the house of Cornelius. Obedience is not always easy. Within God's word to us are areas of challenge to our faith and culture. Our modern society wants us to conform to trends and merchandise labels, but the Christian leader must have the courage to stand alone and buck the trends and contradict tradition in order to be obedient to God's voice. This is no easy matter, but essential if we want to be obedient leaders.

A humble life

Jesus said, *'Blessed are the meek, for they will inherit the earth.'*[3] The psalmist said, *'The LORD ... regards the lowly, but the proud He knows from afar.'*[4]

Learn to walk humbly with the Lord in your daily life. Humility is often missing in Christian leadership. Time spent with God reinforces the fact that any success we may have had is due to His blessing upon our lives. The voice of man will exalt us to the place where we topple and fall. The conscious presence of God will preserve us and help us keep a true perspective of importance.

2. The responsibility of a godly environment at home

The leader's second responsibility after intimacy with God, is the home environment. I cannot emphasise too much the importance of a healthy, happy home. Family environment is primarily the responsibility of the man in the home. The environment should be:

- Godly
- Loving
- Secure
- Honest
- Strife free
- Honourable to the development of all members of the family
- Real
- Relational

Home should be a powerful and supportive place where the leader can relax, laugh and be renewed. I personally thank God for a loving family. For my wife Jenn who has been everything and more than a man could desire, godly, full of wisdom, integrity, love and a great cook! My children Sally and Joel have been a continuous benediction to my life, fully supporting all I have ever done in the ministry. This happy state is worth more than material riches to me. Work at your home environment. It will contribute more to your ministry than you can imagine.

3. The responsibility of leading God's people

The responsibility of the twenty-first century leader is probably best spelt out in Ephesians 4:11–16. Leadership has four main functions:

1. To equip the people (vv. 11–12)
2. To develop maturity in the people (vv. 12–15)
3. To see unity in the church (v. 13)
4. To realise interdependence and mobilisation of the body (vv. 12, 16)

Any leader, who seeks, by the help of the Holy Spirit, to bring about this revolution in the church, will know increase.

4. The responsibility of fulfilling the call of God

Leaders have not only the responsibility of fulfilling God's purpose for their own life, but also of fulfilling God's purpose for the section of Christ's body that they are leading. There is a sense in which these two are almost inseparable. We should note however, that some leaders have moved in God's will to a location of leadership, but have failed on arrival to achieve what God intended them to do.

God has a plan for the people he has called us to lead. Every leader must find what that is and do it by the grace of God. In the Old Testament Saul was appointed king by God, but never achieved God's purpose for Israel or for his own life and family.

Fulfilling God's will	► **Action plan** Write three things that would help you fulfil God's will for your life. 1 . . . . 2 . . . . 3 . . . .

5. The responsibility of the leader to the unregenerate

Twentieth century church leadership, to a large degree, lost the plot due to an over-care of the sheep at the expense of the unregenerate. This resulted in a declining church and an abdication of responsibility to communicate the values of the Christian life to the world. The twenty-first century leader must bring back the priority of Christ's commission to the church if society is to be transformed. Christian leaders find this challenge one of the hardest to fulfil. I have set aside time outside of my world of Christians in order to get closer to non-Christians. I have done this by playing golf with non-Christians and by doing a little secular management training. Both of these areas get me in touch with the people Christ died for.

Leadership functions best when it has settled the issues of this important subject of responsibility firmly into its lifestyle. Only then, will it lead from strength, security and example.

The leader and the non-Christian	▶ **Action plan** Where do you spend time with non-Christians and how often?

The leader's accountability

This is the other side of the coin of credible leadership. We live at a time in history when loyalty and accountability have flown out of the window of society. This has led to everyone doing what seems to be right in their own eyes. This way of thinking is foreign to Christian values. The New Testament teaches that all leadership is accountable. 'Lone Rangers' find no support in the Bible.

Accountability can seem to be threatening, but in seeking to function correctly it is a security and liberation. There are three main areas that a leader's accountability falls into. These are:

Accountability to God
The leader lives first for his Maker and Saviour Jesus Christ. There are times when this accountability conflicts with other areas of accountability. A good example of this is when Peter and John were being commanded to cease teaching in Jesus' name. They answered resolutely, *'We ought to obey God rather than men.'*[5]

In every area of our lives and leadership, from time to time, the big choice faces us. Do we do what God says, or do we do what our emotions, our family, society or church members say? Not easy, but on these issues we must be accountable to God first and foremost. Sooner or later God will always vindicate our trust and obedience to Him.

Accountability to my peers
We have already established that God has set His Ephesians 4 gifts in teams. Leadership in isolation is not a biblical concept. God has placed us in teams so that we can know a strengthening of our gifting and a security for our lives. You may be the leader of leaders, but those leaders you are the leader of can make your leadership better through their counsel. They can also bring safety to your ministry if you listen to them. Good peers love

each other and therefore do not want anything detrimental to happen to any of the team members. Make sure that the peers you hold yourself accountable to are close enough to you to know the truth about your life and ministry.

Here are three good illustrations of submission to peers:

1. Paul and Barnabas to the Jerusalem church leadership in the matter of circumcision.
2. Jerusalem leadership to Peter over Gentile regeneration.
3. *Face values* – an inter-parachurch initiative from the Evangelical Alliance in the UK in 2003, where scores of different organisations held themselves accountable to one another in order to deliver this initiative.

A good team spirit is developed through being open and vulnerable in honesty, trust and love. Jesus built such a good team that the vast majority of those team players were willing to literally die for their Master. People who refuse to be accountable become arrogant and in the end unreachable, in danger of serious long-term failure.

Facing the accountability issue	► **Action plan** Who are you accountable to and how often?

Accountability to the church

Although the New Testament does not teach democracy, it does expect its leadership to be accountable to the church for what it does. Leadership credibility with the people is gained through:

- Integrity
- Strong leadership in difficult circumstances
- Honesty
- Loyalty
- Wisdom
- Perseverance

- Love
- Consultation

You have to earn your spurs in leadership. It does not come overnight, but is strengthened through the daily circumstances and situations of church life. The story is told of the vicar who was moving to another parish after many successful and enjoyable years as the pastor. The day came when he was to leave. He woke up in the morning and looked out of the window to see the entire parish waiting to say goodbye. Tears were flowing down the cheeks of the parishioners, so much so, that the vicar ordered the furniture to be taken off the wagon and placed back in the vicarage. He then sat down and wrote the famous hymn, 'Blessed be the tie that binds our hearts in Christian love'.[6] This man was accountable to his parishioners.

Accountability does not mean you do the bidding of every opinionated person, but it does mean you are prepared to take responsibility for what you do, take advice for what you are about to do, and be open enough to learn from your mistakes, even if it means you have to ask for forgiveness. Through the years of my ministry I have apologised to the church and my team for making leadership mistakes when they have happened.

Some years ago my wife bought me a new wedding ring. I had lost the other when drying my hands in a motorway service station. We were in Turkey for a holiday and thought this was suitable place to replace the lost ring. We looked in many shops without success. One day my eyes fell on a very unusual ring that I liked very much. The ring was attractive to me because of its engraving. The ring had a small diamond in the centre and Roman numerals on each side of the diamond signifying the time between eleven and twelve o'clock. We purchased the ring because the simple symbols on the ring immediately conveyed a message to me about my life and its responsibility and accountability. The message was simple: I am accountable to God, my wife, family and the church for my actions. Whenever I look at the ring I think of these things. The ring also encourages me to make every hour special, as though it were the last before the midnight hour.

When our time on earth is finished, we all will be held accountable to God for the life we have lived and His conclusion on that, is fixed forever.

Is your leadership a bottleneck to the practice of responsibility?

1 ... 2 ... 3 ... 4 ... 5 ... 6 ... 7 ... 8 ... 9 ... 10

Chapter 15

The Honouring Factor

The leader who cannot honour others will not be honoured. Honour is a biblical principle that society too often forgets. The following pages reflect on the importance of honour in the leadership of the church.

For leadership to function properly and effectively, honour is a vital ingredient. Today, this word is not used very often, so it is worth examining its meaning more closely, The Bible literally uses the word to denote beauty, majesty, preciousness, weight, glory and might. The word carries the idea of appreciation together with respect and elevation that stems from achievement, position or responsibility. Where honour is given, there is by definition a submission on the part of the person honouring. Christian leaders in India use the phrase 'the chief guest' when honouring another. This is symbolised in a gesture of praying hands, the seat that is given at the table, the respect that is shown, and sometimes even via a cloak that is placed around the shoulders. They want you to know in no uncertain terms that you are being honoured.

The Western world of leadership can be very egotistic, even though that egoism is cloaked at times in spiritual language. As a result of ego-related confrontations the church, unfortunately, has had more splits than a plank of dry wood.

In this chapter I want us to consider three areas of honour.

The honour of God

The honour of God should be an accepted practice, but we know it is possible to honour God with our lips only.[1] In David's song of praise he said these words, *'Give honour and praise to the* LORD *whose power and beauty fill his holy temple.'*[2] Paul the apostle echoed the same message when he said, *'I pray that honour and glory will always be given to the only God, who lives forever and is the invisible and eternal King! Amen.'*[3] The writer to the Hebrews brings our attention to the honouring of Christ in these words, *'And now that Jesus has suffered and died, he is crowned with glory and honour.'*[4] Of course at the end of the story we see the eternal honour of the Godhead as every knee bows and every tongue confesses Jesus as Lord to the glory of the Father.[5] No credible leader in the church of Jesus Christ can operate unless they practise the honour of Christ in all they do.

If we learn the importance of honouring God, we in turn find a reflection of the importance of the honour principle in daily life. Of course, no one can be honoured as God is, but it is right to honour people. God honours His servants throughout Scripture.

Honouring God	▶ **Action plan** In your busy life, is your honour of God lip service more than true honour? Prayerfully consider this area of your life.

The honour of leadership

Many years ago I was deeply impressed with the actions of one of the pioneers of our movement, a man named John Carter. In the mid sixties the principal of our theological college died suddenly. Mr Carter was called in to fill the gap and a year later was permanently voted in to the position of principal. He served well and a few years later he and a much younger man were the candidates when the position of principal was due for re-election. The votes were counted and it was announced that the young man had won. Mr Carter leaped to his feet and addressed the conference with incredible joy and delight as he congratulated his successor. There was no trace of envy, jealousy, or even disappointment. Mr Carter knew how to rejoice in victory and also in defeat, but more than that, he knew how to honour someone who was his junior. I never forgot that splendid example of honouring another leader and it left a lasting impression in my heart.

The most popular environment for honour, it seems to me, is the funeral service. That person in the coffin either grows angel's wings after death, or they are genuinely and truthfully honoured. The sad thing is that they never get to hear it. We seem to excel in the art of belated honour.

We often find honour most difficult to express to those who are nearest to us. Jesus referred to this when he said, *'Prophets are honoured everywhere, except in their own country.'*[6] This may also suggest a reason why so many leaders prefer an itinerant ministry to a local church ministry? They simply do not feel valued.

Leaders should be honoured for the following reasons:

1. They carry the call of God. To honour them is to honour God. David saw this truth when he was hounded by King Saul and had the opportunity of killing him more than once. He categorically refused to go down that road. On the contrary, he even kept his own soldiers from killing Saul and in the end killed those who had a part in the killing of any of Saul's family. Why? Because he saw Saul as the anointed of God. He did not see him as a perfect man, but as one that God had placed in a position of authority. Therefore David was not going to be party to his removal. Through the years I have watched leaders scheme and through political manoeuvring remove people from office for personal gain. The sad thing is, people who do that are always the losers. You can best honour another person when you are secure in your own position and calling.

2. We honour leaders for the work they do. Paul tells us that they are worthy of double honour.[7] This verse is interesting because it moves from 'lip honour' to material honour. Many leaders seem to live in poor accommodation, drive

old vehicles and receive disgracefully low salaries. I remember as a young minister hearing a deacon say, concerning the way they treated their pastor, 'We keep him poor so that he will be strong in faith.' Where does that come from I ask? Definitely not from God or the Bible! In fact, the way a church cares for their leader is a sign regarding the genuine honour they have for that leader, and may be their real spirituality.

I remember the first time that I travelled to the Holy Land. I wanted my wife to come with me, but we could not afford the plane tickets. The church where I was pastoring decided, without any reference to me, to send my wife to the Holy Land too. They phoned the hospital where she worked, without her knowledge, and changed her holidays! Then they bought the ticket and one week before I was to leave announced what they had done in the Sunday morning service, handing her the ticket there and then! You can imagine the positive affect that had on both my wife and me.

3. Leaders need honouring because they are often in the forefront of the battle and pay an enormous price in terms of enemy attack, discouragement and domestic and material sacrifice. Christian leadership has a pressure all of its own. Not only is it a leadership of people but those people are from the voluntary sector and therefore present not only a higher potential of commitment, but also a much lower degree of availability. This in turn leaves leaders often doing more than they should, particularly in smaller churches.

Honouring leaders	▶ **Action plan** Do you find it hard to honour other leaders and if so, why? Prayerfully seek to answer this challenge.

The honour of one another

The church of the twenty-first century must be a church where all are honoured. Leaders can fall into the trap of thinking that they are the only ones who should be honoured. A church functions best when all are honoured. This starts in the home where the husband honours the wife and children and vice versa.[8] It is sad that this often is lacking in the leader's home. If it is lacking there, how can it be modelled in the church?

Good leadership, both publicly and privately, will honour all people within their congregation at the appropriate times. I think it is good to be a general encourager of people. Say 'thank you' often, or 'I appreciate you'. Talk to others of the good that people are doing. Paul reminds us, *'Love each other as brothers and sisters and honour others more than you do yourself.'*[9] The apostle amplifies the principle of honour when he explains how the body works harmoniously together. He deliberately picks out the weaker or less profiled member and says, *'For those members of the body that we think to be less honourable, upon these we bestow more abundant honour . . . '*[10] Here Paul is going out of his way to bring honour to the most marginalised person in the congregation.

I spent some time with a most unassuming man who had achieved success in his chosen field of expertise. He was very popular on the after dinner speech circuit. He told me that he was fascinated by the fickleness and shallowness of many leaders in the secular world. He told me that he often arrives early for his appointment and always dresses down. In fact he often looks like the hotel electrician as he walks around with his cables and laptop. He said CEOs and directors often ignore him and treat him very poorly because they don't know who he is and assume he is a nobody. When he finally introduces himself, the same people are totally embarrassed and shower him with respect, but the damage has already been done. Why? Because leadership very often is more concerned with the honour of those that can bring benefit to them, rather than with respecting the principle of true honour.

Many years ago I spent a great deal of time in the Houses of Parliament. I met many MPs and Lords. The thing that amazed me was the almost total obsession these people had with themselves. Nearly every conversation was a platform for self-promotion. I thank God that there were a few who were void of such egotism.

Honouring one another teaches us that honour is not just a hierocracy thing, but a value of life. I observed a very fine young leader working overtime to get his PA to understand the importance of honouring him. She worked herself inside out to give him everything that he needed in terms of her PA work, to the degree that behind the scenes she would break down and cry. The young leader gave very little if any honour back to his PA. Do you think that this PA was going to value this young leader? Would she speak highly of him to others? Of course not! In failing to give reciprocal honour the young leader lost his case and in the end will lose his PA.

Where are you on the honouring scale? Are you a bottleneck in this matter?

Honouring the people	▶ **Action plan** Analyse your conversations and tributes to see where you give most honour. If the ordinary person is missing, then correct it quickly.

Is your leadership a bottleneck to the honouring factor?

1 ... 2 ... 3 ... 4 ... 5 ... 6 ... 7 ... 8 ... 9 ... 10

SECTION FOUR

Passing the Baton

Chapter 16

Transitional Leadership

Evangelical history shows that Christians have not been good at transitional leadership, that is, leading from one phase to the next. Churches have had to repair the damage after leaders have either died or moved on. Why have we failed? What must be done to correct this failure? This chapter offers practical insights on this matter.

During the depression of the twenties the Weaver family lived in the Forest of Dean, Gloucestershire, England. They were just a poor family. The father, Clifford was on the dole. Just ten shillings (50p) a week was all they had to support the four family members, father, mother May, daughter Joan and son Fred.

At breakfast one morning (which was just two rounds of toast each with a scraping of margarine), just before Clifford said grace, mother asked the question, 'What are we going to do? Our children need better food and new clothes.' Clifford made no direct reply, but proceeded to give thanks for the food with a simple concluding request for more food and clothes. After they had eaten, while mother was clearing the table, there was a knock at the front door. She went and answered it. There stood a poorly dressed man. He said, 'Lady, I'm hungry, could you please give me something to eat?' Mother said, 'All we have left is some toast, but come on in and you are welcome to it.'

The man entered and sat down at the table. Immediately, he began to talk of the wonders and glories of God. The family sat there in rapt attention. Mother toasted the last of the bread and gave it to him. With head bowed, he gave thanks to God and then ate the toast. Later, he rose to his feet and thanked father Clifford and mother for their hospitality, and then lifting his hands to heaven pronounced a prophetic blessing on the family. This blessing was then extended to future generations of children.

On completion of his prayer, mother showed him to the door and he left with another word of thanks. Mother came back into the kitchen to tidy up the table and chairs. As she pushed the chair that the man had been sitting on back under the table, she shouted, 'Oh, look Dad!' On the chair were pound notes in mint condition. Mum counted them, twenty in all. Father Clifford jumped to his feet and dashed to the front door and then into the road to call the man back. The family lived in a quiet road that was straight and long. Father Clifford gazed up and down the road looking for the man, but without success. He had vanished.

Father Clifford came back into the house and said, 'Children, God has sent an angel here today in answer to our prayer for food and clothes.'

For two or three days there seemed to be a holy atmosphere in the home. From that day on, the Weaver family never wanted for food or clothing. God provided miraculously through the depression years until they were able to provide for themselves.

The purposes, provisions and fulfilments of God's promises are quite amazing. Sixty-eight years later (2004) the future generations that the angel prophesied about number five children in all – three to Fred and Dora: Paul, Joyce, and Hazel, each serving God in church leadership, and two to Joan and George, each serving God. Now Fred has eight grandchildren who are all serving God and Joan, who has since died, has three grandchildren who are also serving God.

From generation to generation, God is faithful. In an amazing way the grace and salvation of God has passed down through the generations of my family until this present day. I am the recipient of transitional blessing.

It is said of King David that, *'After he had served his own generation by the will of God, he fell asleep.'*[1] It is important to observe what David did in God's will when he served his generation. Part of that service was to appoint his successor. After David came to the throne and joined Israel and Judah together as one nation under one king, he had a clear yet incredible message from God. The prophet Nathan recognised the harmonious life of David with the will of God and said, 'Do whatever is in your heart.' The word of God went on to explain a profound truth about God's dwelling place that we are only now discovering in the church today.[2] In addition to these things, God gives David a generational blessing. The building of the Temple is going to be denied to David, but his son Solomon will be his successor and have the joy of executing that building project.

God is always one step ahead of where we are. The secret is to tap into that step. Raise your 'tomorrow' team today. We are given this important message after David's death concerning his success in transitional leadership:

> *'So David slept with his fathers, and was buried in the city of David. And the days that David reigned over Israel were forty years: seven years reigned he in Hebron, and thirty and three years reigned he in Jerusalem. Then sat Solomon upon the throne of David his father; and his kingdom was established greatly.'*
>
> (1 Kings 2:10–12, AV)

You cannot control the business from the grave, so make provision for the business to be taken care of before you retire or die.

This raises the issue of how leaders are appointed in the local church. Historically leaders were trained by institutional process to lead churches they had never been a part of. They came by invitation and were often compared with other leaders. Then there would be a competitive vote, a million miles in my opinion, from the Word of God. I remember being called 'with a view' as it was termed in those days, to the church in Scunthorpe in 1970. Historically they had always asked a few leaders to come 'with a view', before picking the one they wanted. I was not comfortable with this procedure and thank God neither were the church after many years of leaders coming and going. They printed a small card which read: 'Please pray that we will find the right man to be our pastor.' This was given to all the members for daily prayer. Eighteen months earlier God had spoken to me with the message that one day I would go to Scunthorpe to be their pastor. I immediately shared this with my fiancé, thinking it would be many years in the future, so we put it to the back of our minds. The local church in Scunthorpe felt that God had placed my name in their hearts, even though I had never been to Scunthorpe in my life, and they made the invitation. The church voted for my appointment and the rest, as they say, is history.

The way leaders are appointed to churches today is in the embryonic stage of change. I predict that transitional leadership will increasingly be in the ascendancy. The next twenty years could reveal a major shift whereby church leadership rises from the ranks of the local church and not from the theological colleges of our lands. This will inevitably challenge the way we train and recognise leadership in the future. This does not mean that leaders of the future will not have exposure to theological colleges, but it will mean that their training will come via a local leadership agenda. This agenda will include a position for the trainee in the local leadership team.

Larger churches today are in an advantageous position of being able to draw training from anywhere in the world. Some of this training is done through distance learning, some by secondment for degree programmes, some by attending conferences, and some by studying larger church structures. We live in a global village that is enabling different approaches to leadership training to emerge.

Where did you come from?	► **Action plan** How did you come to lead the church where you are and in hindsight was that the best way?

What is transitional leadership?

Transitional leadership is a process of recognition, training, and release of leadership within a local church or organisation.

It should be stated at the outset, that this process should not be viewed as the only way of providing future leaders. Neither should it be seen as failure proof or an impediment to receiving leadership from outside of the local church.

Biblical illustrations of this concept can be traced from Moses to Paul. The training of Joshua by Moses for the leadership role of Israel was achieved by Moses taking Joshua aside from the rest of the leaders and teaching him God's purposes for his life. He exposed him to a deeper revelation of God up the mountain and affirmed the vision of the Promised Land in his heart and before the people of Israel. Elijah follows a similar pattern as he mentors Elisha, through a variety of testing and instruction to the place where he is capable of wearing the mantle of Elijah. In the case of Jesus, He provides not one, but eleven leaders for the early church. Paul follows in these footsteps to train and equip a number of younger men for office, probably best exampled in Timothy whom he calls his son. Transitional leadership is not a new phenomenon, but a well-documented and practised procedure.

Why transitional leadership?

More damage has been done to the local church through a lack of leadership continuity than most other things. I remember when I moved to be the leader of New Life church in Scunthorpe, Lincolnshire, England in 1970. The church had had a new minister every two years on average. One deacon said to me after I had been leading the church for just eighteen months, 'So I suppose you will be leaving soon?' I looked him in the eye and said, 'I will be here when you have gone', and I was.

Unconnected leadership succession provides years of wasted opportunity for growth. People are denied continuity of vision, teaching and security of leadership. People are denied on-the-job training and future development. The leadership skills in the congregation are often lost to the next leader and fatherhood and mentoring are lost to the congregation.

I know there are also possible disadvantages to long-term ministry. These can be, rut-mentality, lack of vision, control, frustration and predictability. However, overall there is much more to be said for long-term ministry and especially where it moves towards transitional leadership through home-grown leaders.

In a nutshell, most of the growing churches in the world are enjoying the continuity of long-term leadership together with some method of transitional leadership: Saddleback, Willow Creek, Bogotá and Seoul in Korea. These churches echo the New Testament process originated in the Jerusalem, Antioch and Ephesus churches.

This third millennium is ripe for the restoration of this vital dimension of leadership understanding. We have to raise our 'tomorrow' team today. We cannot lead the church from the grave.[3]

How do we train our successors?

The relay race requires a different paradigm from the race where individuals run for themselves. You have to think differently. You have to think as a team. The team knows that each runner is different; they each run at different speeds. These speeds can be used strategically to your advantage in the race. Every runner has to keep running if the team is to achieve victory. The hand-over is vital. How you pass the baton can win or lose the race. All the team rejoice in victory on the same podium, and if they lose, they all work to improve their performance for a better day.

A well-oiled team knows that they can run faster over 400 metres as a team, than each of them can run 100 metres as individuals. The 2004 Olympics illustrated this principle well. The 4 × 100 metre relay final should have been won by the Americans. They had the individual winner's medals and the silver and bronze in the 100 metres race. The British were the losers in the same race. Yet, when it came to the 4 × 100 metre relay, the British team, made up of losers won! Why? Because they were better on the day at *transition*; they handed the baton on perfectly and won. The Americans came back however in the 4 × 400 relay to win by improving their baton passing. The lesson is clear: losers can be winners and winners can be winners, *if* they know how to pass the baton well.

The Americans in the world of athletics have worked hard at

developing the power of team. They have discovered that through the process of team training they get a higher individual performance rate than when athletes train on their own. The psychology is simply, 'We perform better when we think and work for team than we do when we work for our own ends.' This idea has been extended to embrace athletes who are just beneath Olympic standards. They have found that after training with an Olympic team they make a rapid improvement up to the standard of the rest of the team. And even though they may run alone in their sphere of athletic expertise, in the back of their mind they are running for the team. In some churches in the world this lesson is being learned. The next stage however, is to see the extension of a highly efficient and productive team transfer its strengths to the next generation of leadership.

The following comments are offered from my own experience of transitional leadership in 2001/2. This experience was not flawless, but holds sufficient wisdom to be helpful to the subject material in this chapter.

I came to the church in Scunthorpe, England as a young married man after working for nearly five years with a successful senior leader in Sunderland, England. Scunthorpe was a small town of about 50,000 people with no real catchment area to draw on and was monopolised by a steel complex.

The church known as the 'Pentecostal church' was traditional, but quite well known throughout our denomination because of the many leaders that had led the church and for its musical talent. It was a very strongly democratic church in the hands of a deaconate. So much so that you could not even buy a pair of curtains without first taking a vote! My salary was frugal and therefore not really enough to live on, so my wife practised midwifery to supplement our income. God was gracious and blessed the work, even though I was operating in a very traditional style of leadership, which was the only one I knew and the style I had been trained in. Quite simply, I did most things, but this was the way it was in those days. By the year 1980 we had moved into a brand new building costing a quarter of a million pounds. We had put a leadership team together with eldership, even though in hindsight this was more a group of leaders than a team. The church had grown to over two hundred and things were rolling nicely when all of a sudden the town was hit with a blow that nearly sunk us. Scunthorpe suffered a massive reduction in employment in the steel industry from 21,000 employees to just 6,000. It almost reduced us to a ghost town. People left the area because there were no jobs; others took early retirement payouts with no prospect of employment again. It was not until nearly five years later that any real significant investment was made in the town.

Through those lean years we had to rebuild the church and at the same time we moved into 'small group' ministry. We ran 'house groups' for fifteen years. We were ahead of most churches in this practice as 'house groups' were looked on by many as a distraction from the devil because of the division they had caused in other churches where they had been introduced. We learned many lessons through the development of these groups. One lesson was, small groups were not mini congregations and therefore should not be conducted as such. They required a different sort of leader and an outward looking objective for their purpose.

It was during the mid-eighties that I also began to be involved in the national scene of Assemblies of God, being elected to their Executive Council and later becoming one of the assistants to the General Superintendent. The beginning of the nineties saw a major shake up in my own life concerning the issue of church and how it should really function. This caused me to introduce cell ministry to the church and reappraise the way I led the church and operated as a leader. I sought to involve my leaders more in function, worked to train more leaders, and mobilised the church to mission. In 1995 I became the General Superintendent while still leading the church in Scunthorpe, and in the year 2000 I felt God tell me to hand the church over to one of the younger leaders in my team.

I shared this with the team and the young man. After prayer and much conversation, it was agreed that Russell Westfield should become my successor. Although Russ had grown up in the church, he was the newest member of my leadership team. We announced to the church that we would transition the leadership of the church from me to Russ, but gave no handover date. We decided that we would take as long as it needed for this transitional period to reach its completion. I met with Russ every week and shared many things; I sought to equip him as much as I was able. After about sixteen months we felt it was time to announce the date of handover. Two months later Russ took charge as senior leader and appointed his own team, some of whom were from my team. I took no official office in the church at my own request, so that Russ could process his vision more easily. As I write this book, two years have gone by and I can see many changes. There is continual growth in the church, and the values remain the same. I gaze upon a church that is steadily finding new expressions of development, with familiar marks from the past. Has it all been easy? No! Are there lessons to learn from it? Absolutely. What are those lessons?

Lessons learned

Transitional leadership is a team paradigm. It plays to the strengths of the team not just those of gifted individuals. It is carried out with the long-term positions that the team players will occupy in mind, including that which the current senior leader will hold in the future. This means that although there will be a distinctiveness about the *new* senior leader, there will be a sense of affirmation regarding the values, purpose and vision of the church that does not need to be learned because the DNA of the team and the church has already been imparted by the former senior leader.

Eyes to see the new leadership
None of us have it all and none of us will be able to function in our office always. My advice is to hand on before you lose it and overstay both your welcome and your divine time allocation. Move on to the next stage of your ministry. God has a purpose for every minute of your life, so don't worry.

I had watched Russ develop over many years from a young musician of fifteen years of age, who took my place on the piano as the pianist for the youth choir, through to being the church's music director and youth leader. It had been my joy to open doors for his ministry through those years and now to see him become my successor. The important qualities I was looking for were fourfold; a godly man, a tomorrow thinker, a man of faith, and a man of loyalty. Russ had all of these qualities.

These qualities were in Moses' successor Joshua too. Joshua was a man of faith, one of the twelve spies who said, 'We can take the land.' His vision was for the Promised Land, not the merry-go-round of the wilderness. Joshua had been schooled up the mountain with Moses and had learnt how to communicate with God. He also had a clear mandate from God for his leadership.[4]

Good leadership can always see beyond the function of its own gifting. Russ worked with me for twenty-five years. In those years I could see the potential of what he could become before others even had an inkling of it. Can you see your successor yet?

Time for mentoring

I have always sought to give opportunity for the development of people's giftings by training them, injecting faith and competency into their ministry and then releasing them to the calling of God in their lives. During the years of my leadership at Scunthorpe we were able to see twenty-five people go into full-time service as leaders.

Having said all of this, I only wish that I had always known what I now know about the subject of mentoring. For people of my generation this is a difficult aspect of ministry to develop. Mentoring is the depositing of experience into a less experienced life. It is about the development of the gifts of the mentored and not about duplicating your gifts in them. It is a commitment to their success. It calls for an honesty, deep love and sound relationship together with an undaunted belief in that person.

Before Russ became senior leader we spent many hours, weeks and months building his abilities and confidence for the job he was to assume. After he was inducted as the senior leader, I met him every month for the next year to talk through the work, his progress and problems. A successor requires support and wisdom. Sometimes they think they know it all. There are times when they need to prove they are now the leader. The predecessor has to take all of this into account as they support their successor. There are times to speak and times to keep silent. During this period of the successor finding their true security in leadership, which can take years, the predecessor can at times, seem at best a problem and at worst an enemy.

The wisdom to discern – your successor
A church requires different gifts at different times at the helm of the leadership team, but all senior leaders should be more than a pastoral gift. Historically, the local church has looked for a pastoral figure as their leader. But a purely pastoral gift is more maintenance-orientated than progressive, hence the reason why the average numerical strength of local churches globally is below fifty. The future will reveal the importance of a senior leader being apostolic in function.

We had excellent leaders, teachers and pastors in the team at New Life church, but my successor had to have that apostolic dimension that could see the whole picture and develop people for the future and for expansion. The successor is not therefore necessarily the one who has worked the longest with us, but the one that fits the criteria in line with the above comments for the next section of the journey.

The faith to believe
The successor may not always be the obvious choice of everyone.

I remember Wynne Lewis, the former leader of the famous Kensington Temple church in London, telling the story of his successor, Colin Dye. When he approached his leadership and said Colin was to be his successor, none of that leadership could see what Wynne could see in the unknown Colin.

The job of the senior leader in office is to prepare the way for the new person to be accepted. The senior leader should be able to see what others can't. I chose Russ because I believe God showed me he was the right man, even though his qualities were not fully appreciated by those around at that time, or properly developed. I remember when we announced the name of Russ as my successor to the church, there were those who came to me and asked why another member of my team was not going to be the senior leader. This other member of my team had worked with me the longest of all my full-time leaders. His loyalty to me was without question. He had carried the pastoral responsibilities of the church for a number of years and the people loved him. People always love the people who visit them the most. Although he carried a pastoral heart, he did not have the apostolic gift to take the church forward. Explaining this to him was not easy, but his gracious character and the clear recognition of what his gift was, enabled him to positively and genuinely accept my decision and fully support Russ in every way. This he has continued to do to an exemplary degree.

Before we brought the name of Russ to the church, I had brought his name to the leadership team privately. There was at first surprise that I was handing over the church, and then each member had to come to terms with the name I had nominated. I asked them to pray and to talk about the matter on their own, without me being present. I gave them three months for this process. I wanted them to have the same conviction as myself. We moved forward only when we had all agreed. God commands His blessing where brothers dwell together in unity.

The pace of change
How long does it take for the transition? The simple answer is, as long as it takes. Every church has a different pace at which it makes change. If you are in a city, the likelihood is that you will be able to make changes more quickly, because people live in an environment where generally change happens faster. If you live in a rural area, the pace of change will be much slower. All leaders should learn the pace of change their church can sustain and having learnt this, pace the handover carefully. Remember, leaders move at a faster pace than the congregation. Our transition took eighteen months from the leadership discussions, to the congregation announcement, to Russ working alongside me, to Russ leading with my support, and finally to the handover and Russ being the official senior leader.

The confidence to let go
It is not easy to let go. I thought I would be the leader of New Life until I retired. Your life and the emotions of many years are

wrapped up in this experience. These are like *your* children; you have nursed them, dedicated them, married them, dedicated their kids, buried their relatives, walked the dark roads with them, rejoiced in their joy, and wept with them in their sorrows. You can't let go without deep feelings of emotion.

What are the problems to letting go? How do you let go without opting out? This was a big one for me. I was still a member of the church; my wife was still part of the leadership of the church; I wanted the church to prosper, but I had no official position in the church. The last thing that I wanted was to get in the way of Russ. Subconsciously, I felt myself wondering who I was. I knew who I was in my role as General Superintendent and outside of my local church, but here in the local church, who was I? Russ verbally said some nice things about me, but how and where was I to function? It was at this point that I realised that for all of my ministerial life I had functioned in two areas of authority, namely the authority of my calling as an Ephesians 4:11 gift, and also in the authority of my office as senior leader in the local church. That office was no longer there, but my gifting remained. How was I to operate this 'throne' gift in the local church? Should I wait for the invitation from my successor, or do I just operate my gift? I believe that we must always obey and respect our leaders. I have always expected this of those in the churches I have led. I therefore sat quietly and only ministered when asked. This was difficult and one day when Russ called the leaders out to pray for people at the front, my wife went and I stayed seated. When we got home my wife said, 'Why didn't you come out and pray for the people?' I replied, 'Russ didn't ask me.' It was at this point that I realised the trouble I was in. I went to Russ and said, 'I have a problem' and then explained it to him. He said, 'I have a problem too. How do I pastor you?' We laughed, and sought to deal with the problem. It is never easy. We still wrestle with these areas of operation.

Another problem is how to let go without becoming the hand in the puppet. There is nothing worse than the new leader having to contend with an overbearing predecessor trying to run the church *through* the new leader. The dilemma and tension is, when do you share your experience, wisdom and wider perspective on the church, and when do you keep your mouth shut? A parallel might be that delicate period as a parent when your child is in-between being a teenager and an adult. You know if you tell the child too strongly what they ought to do, you will lose their ear and yet you don't want to see them fall down unnecessarily. I think leaders who stay on in churches that they have led face this tension to some degree or other. Of course when we do say something, we must make sure that we are truly helping the situation and not merely passing on our opinion, honed by the bias of our style of leadership. This would be totally unacceptable.

Another problem area is how to let go without becoming the leader of division. Every predecessor will have disquieted people come to them. It will happen either in the first few months, or after the new leader has had their honeymoon period. Normally the people that come to you are from the older section of the church and those who have experienced your leadership the longest. Very often the problems they are experiencing are to do with the change in their lives resulting from moving from one style of leadership to another. I have had people come to me hoping that I would share their pain or agree with their disquiet. The easiest thing at this point is to fall into the trap of going on an ego trip and bathing in the bubbles of a resurrected recognition. The worst thing that any leader can do is to become party to division. Predecessors must always support the new leader unless that new leader is teaching error, and then they should take that up with the leader direct and the leadership team.

The opportunity to function
Every member of the church is called to function in the local body. So both leaders must find their level of function in the new picture.

The role of the new leader
The new leader of the church must operate as the person God has made him. His style may be different, but the spirit and values should carry the continuity of the purpose of transitional leadership. His experience will be less, therefore requiring help,

not dominance, and lots of encouragement. His initial period of leadership will be to find his feet, and he may be threatened with a sense of intimidation from his predecessor. Sometimes the new leader will ignore his father in the faith as he finds his identity as the new leader. Predecessors should not view this as rejection.

The role of the old leader

Am I on the shelf or in the plan? The former leader must find a role in which he can serve the new leader. Before the transition is made, a new role sould be agreed for the predecessor, something that will be fulfilling and something that gives him an identity; something perhaps quite different from his previous role. The former leader must understand their authority within that new role, and must not assume that it carries the same level of authority as the role of senior leader did.

If you are in this position, it will help you to eliminate the frustration of not knowing where you fit. Understand too your role as an older leader. You are the father of the house. No one can take that away from you, you have earned it, so enjoy it. In the natural world, the role of the grandparent is a privileged one and quite different from that of a parent. You are also a member in the church which takes some adjusting to, so be patient with yourself and others. If you have a role or position outside of the local church, then seek the support and release of your local church to that ministry. Every month Jim Musgrave, a wonderful member of the leadership of New Life, includes my ministry in the intercessors prayer diary. This means that over thirty-five people in the church bring my ministry schedule before God each day, which means so much to me.

There is pain for the predecessor that demands an honest self-appraisal. I have already talked about the question, 'Who am I in the new era?' There is also the frustration of contrasting leadership styles that your successor will bring. What about the place of your wife in the new regime? What is her new role, her identity, and what does that mean within the church and the home? For example, my wife moved from first lady, to a member of the leadership team. She had looked to me all her life for vision in regard to the church and now she had to look to another leader. This meant that she knew the plans for the next stage of the church's journey before I did. Add to this her vast experience of church leadership – how does all this fit into the new leadership era?

Despite all these questions, the role of the retiring leader is to serve the new leader before God, the people, and his family. This could be summarized as follows: our attitude must be like the Master who washed the feet of His future leaders.[5] Serve the leader and the church with your gifts. Jesus served the church through the gifts He gave to it.[6] Always be loyal and be an encouragement to everyone who participates in the ministry of the church. Always love the people of God. And this will keep your spirit from any bitterness.

The joy of transition

Jesus was able to endure the pain of transition, because of the joy of seeing people like us in fellowship with the Creator. Transition is full of joyous moments when we watch the development of the new leader and those who serve him. We see their success and rest in the excitement of the extension of the kingdom, no matter who is the leader of the local church. Enjoy the success of your successor more than your own success.

I remember sitting on the front row at my mother's funeral and looking along the line of my immediate and extended family as they were worshipping God. I thought to myself, 'Yes Mum, you have invested your life through prayer, love and support and we are your success.'

There are some lovely prophetic verses in the Psalms about the church growing, maturing and everyone counting. They read:

> 'Good people will prosper like palm trees and they will grow strong like cedars of Lebanon. They will take root in your house, LORD God and they will do well [be discipled]. They will be like trees that stay healthy and fruitful, even when they are old [longevity of usefulness]. And they will say about you, "The LORD always does right! God is our mighty rock."' (Psalm 92:12–15, CEV)

The end accolade is always glory to God. To end one's life with a sweet spirit is to die with honour. David served his generation in the will of God.

> **'Our success is in our successors.'**

Facing the transitional challenge	▶ **Action plan** Who are you training for succession? Don't leave it too late. Begin now to think about the future in all of its ramifications.

Is your leadership a bottleneck to transitional leadership?

1 ... 2 ... 3 ... 4 ... 5 ... 6 ... 7 ... 8 ... 9 ... 10

Chapter 17

The Leader's Final Mile

What we do at the end of our ministry can have a profound bearing on what we have done previously, and ultimately on our heavenly reward. This last chapter remembers that our earthly journey is only a short walk compared to eternity. The lesson is, 'Make sure you get it right in time, because there is no other time to get it right.'

In 2002 there was a competitor in the London marathon by the name of Michael Watson. Watson had been a British champion boxer but had been seriously injured and had to retire. He worked hard on his recovery and moved from being confined to a wheelchair to being able to walk, albeit with very restrictive movement. Watson started well. But because of his limited movement did not finish the marathon until *five days* later. The organisers rallied on that fifth day to re-erect the finishing staging and placed the tape across the road. Hundreds turned out to cheer the man who had overcome his disability to finish the race with honour.

All of us have a final mile before we meet our Creator. Very often that last mile can turn sour in the life of a leader. The importance of finishing well cannot be underestimated. A lifetime of hard work can be lost in the final stretch towards home.

The Greek word *teleios* carries an important challenge for all leaders. It means 'to complete'. It's not where you have come from that matters, but where you finish that counts. Guided missiles have an inbuilt mechanism that is designed to finish well. You can launch them from any site, but the missile will correct itself to concentrate on the target and finish well.

It is a sad fact that only 1 in 10 people who enter the ministry are still in the ministry at 65 years of age, many of whom become causalities before the tape. Jesus said,

> *'Suppose one of you wants to build a tower. Will he not first sit down and estimate the cost to see if he has enough money to complete it? For if he lays the foundation and is not able to finish it, everyone who sees it will ridicule him, saying, "This fellow began to build and was not able to finish."'*
>
> (Luke 14:28–30, NIV)

Fellow leader, as you read this last chapter prepare for a good end. You might be a young leader who is living for the moment and the last mile may seem an eternity away, but believe me, you will arrive there sooner than you realise and what you are learning now will shape for you that last mile.

The Belbin Management Test always reveals the scarcity of a vital team member that is called by Belbin, a 'Finisher'. The knock-on effect of this scarcity is that many a grand vision was never realised because there was no one there to complete it.

The Bible says of Moses, *'Moses finished the work'*.[1] The following pages highlight four good finishers that I trust will prepare and encourage you for your last mile.

Zerubbabal the builder

Zechariah's prophetic word to Zerubbabal to build the second temple was quite daunting. After all, who could match the excellence and magnificence of Solomon's Temple? Yet, this faithful leader had this prophetic word spoken over him, *'Zerubbabal laid the foundation for the temple, and he will complete it.'*[2] 'To complete it' simply means, 'to finish it, to cut off, to end the matter'.

Within the prophet's word to Zerubbabel were some amazing promises. First, Zerubbabel would be a *success* – that meant he would begin and finish the work God had commissioned him to do. God has built success into every calling. God's word to Jeremiah illustrates this, *'I will bless you with a future filled with hope – a future of success, not of suffering.'*[3] Success of course is not measured solely through human eyes, but more importantly through divine eyes. I remember travelling to Bogotá in the mid nineties to look at César Castellanos' church. One day I was in conversation with César and asked him this question, 'Why do you think revival has come to your land?' Without hesitation, he referred back to a missionary who had laboured for many years in the country, and who died with no seeming success. 'That man,' said César, 'prayed and laid spiritual foundations in this country that we today are being blessed from.'

Don't be afraid of the word 'success', it simply means, 'the favourable outcome of something attempted'. Prophetic fulfilment reveals God authenticity. The finished work showed God's hand was in it all. Completion is in God's strategy for our lives.

Beginnings must not be despised. God rejoices over our beginnings.[4] The AV uses the words *'small things'*. We are very good at being attracted to success when it has arrived, but often blind to the work of the Holy Spirit at the beginning of a work. Jesus talked about a mustard seed being very small, but growing in size to shelter the birds of the air. Through the years I have witnessed the acorns of life becoming the mighty oaks. One such story would be that of 'Alpha' the excellent outreach programme started in Holy Trinity Brompton, London. This started out as just another local church initiative that could so easily have been lost in the aisles of a local church, but someone believed in its potential and invested heavily in launching Alpha to the Christian world at large. Today Alpha is being used in scores of countries with great success. Don't miss the potential of the acorn; small things grow into big things. The things you have planted in your earlier years of ministry will blossom to success as the years roll by.

Another point worth registering is the fact that 'God is watching'.[5] The eyes of the Lord are upon us all the time – at the beginning of our endeavour, in the middle, and also at the end. Cliff Richards made a hit song out of this truth. It was entitled, 'God is watching us'. I know sometimes the eyes of the Lord can have a negative effect upon us, but I believe if we seek to do what is right, the eyes of the Lord watching over us, can become the most positive encouragement on our journey. The old negro song got it right, 'I sing because I'm happy, I sing because I free, His eye is on the sparrow and I know He watches me.'

Your work as a leader will be accomplished only by the work of the Spirit. God says to you, *'I am the* LORD *All-powerful. So don't depend on your own power or strength, but on my Spirit.'*[6] This journey is not just about us, but our relationship with God and His resources. When we work in relationship with God, we become people of the Spirit. The Zechariah text continues saying, *'These branches are the two chosen leaders who stand beside the Lord of all the earth.'*[7] The Hebrew text has: 'people of oil' or 'sons of oil'. Zerubbabel and Joshua became the 'sons of oil' (leaders in partnership with the Holy Spirit) for the building of the Temple. That anointing was able to level the mountains and erect the purpose of God in the nation at that time. Zerubbabel was destined to complete the work and walk the last mile of his ministry with joy. Ezra tells us that this second temple was completed and its glory was greater than the first.[8] If you keep going in the power of God's Spirit, you will succeed.

Foundation and completion	▶ **Action plan** Look back over your life and rejoice over all the things that you have played a part in. Rest in the realisation that it was not wasted.

Solomon the Temple builder

The second illustration of a finished work comes in Solomon's reign.

David's instructions to Solomon regarding the building of the Temple were very clear. He said,

> *'David also said to Solomon his son, "Be strong and courageous, and do the work. Do not be afraid or discouraged, for the* LORD

God, my God, is with you. He will not fail you or forsake you until all the work for the service of the temple of the LORD is finished. The divisions of the priests and Levites are ready for all the work on the temple of God, and every willing man skilled in any craft will help you in all the work. The officials and all the people will obey your every command." '

(1 Chronicles 28:20–21, NIV)

These verses have been important to me on the journey of denominational reformation within Assemblies of God in the UK. When you are seeking to lead people and change their ways of thinking and practice, it can be very lonely at times. Solomon would have felt this, but he kept going. When Solomon finished the work it seems that God wanted to impress this success on future generations by recording it in many places in the Bible. God reiterates the phrase over and over again, 'Solomon finished'. Seven years after starting the Temple building was complete.[9] Then Solomon's house followed, which took another thirteen years to complete.[10] Solomon earned the commendation that he finished everything God gave him to do.

What were the qualities that Solomon had to exhibit in order to finish his work? Solomon had to be strong and courageous. This is an inner strength and courage that is not dependent upon circumstances, but on a deep conviction of what is required in your calling; you have the ability to complete the task. Solomon had to have a faith equal to the task. He was told not to be afraid of the size of the task. There is a big difference in building terms between the tabernacle in the wilderness and the Temple in Jerusalem.

The size or difficulty of the job is not the issue. The issue is the size of your God and His releasing word of command.

As a young minister my first two tasks in the realm of believing God for resources was first for my weekly salary, which God miraculously met, and secondly for an organ that we needed, but had no money to pay for. In the early seventies, a Hammond organ was a state of the art in Pentecostal circles! Prior to me becoming their pastor the church had saved for three years and was still nowhere near finding even the deposit for an organ. I remember talking to a friend of mine who was a brilliant organist and also the manager of a music shop. I asked him to bring a Hammond organ and play it in the church for the Sunday meetings and to see what the people would think. He came and played brilliantly. After the evening service he said to me, 'If you want, you can keep the organ for three months and if you have the money at the end of that, it's yours.' At that time the church governance was democratic. This meant that everything went to the congregation for a decision and nothing was purchased through hire-purchase agreements. 'Owe no one anything' was the motto. I told him to leave the organ with us. I remember coming to the Tuesday night prayer meeting and the deacons giving me a very grave look. 'Why have we still got the organ?' they asked with very serious looking faces. I replied with the good news that, 'The organ is ours!' The deacons looked in utter bewilderment; they knew the matter had not come before the deaconate or the church meeting. I continued, '. . . if we pay for it within three months.' Silence pervaded. I then said, 'I believe we will have the money in three months.' The money came in before the three months were up. From such small beginnings of faith, God enabled me to see a quarter of a million pound project as my next task, followed by a two-and-a-half million pound project at the beginning of the nineties, and eventually the task of denominational transformation. Every victory won is a step to a greater task.

Solomon had to be sure that God was with him. David's words to his son were to bring him this assurance. How affirming to know that when the chips are down, naturally speaking, God is with us and that He turns the tables around and puts us in the majority.

Solomon had to come to know the God he served. God is faithful to provide all we need for the task. We can see this in these words, '. . . *the various groups of priests and Levites that would serve in the temple. Others with skills of every kind would volunteer, and the leaders and the entire nation would be at Solomon's command.*'[11]

Solomon finally had the joy of experiencing God's glory come down on his labours. What a conclusion!

What is God leading you to complete?	▶ **Action plan** The last mile can be the most difficult. The task now may be smaller than those you have already participated in, but it is no less significant. Complete it with joy.

Jesus the Saviour

Jesus was a man who was single-minded in the matter of accomplishing His Father's will. His mission was to do His Father's. He set His face as a flint towards Jerusalem. He kept the major thing, the major thing. His 'time management' was an hourly one: 'My hour has not yet come.' His energy came from the Holy Spirit, the word, prayer and obedience. This is illustrated in the words, *'Jesus said to them, "My food is to do the will of Him who sent Me, and to finish His work."'* [12]

During the last mile of His journey, He knew He had succeeded when He said, *'I have finished the work which You have given Me to do.'* [13] Jesus uses the word *teleioo* meaning 'to complete' or 'to perfect' everything that was required to finish the assignment.

Later on, Jesus declared His success with confidence before the Father, people, and the devil, at the worst possible time as far as circumstances were concerned, in the words, *'It is finished!'* [14] This word 'finished' is *teleo* meaning, 'to bring to an end'. Jesus brought it to an end. He said, 'No man takes my life, I lay it down.'

In the awesome final words of an old hymn we say, 'What a Saviour!' His victory has emancipated all who believe. This is the God we serve. I remember looking at this incredible victory of Christ some years ago and thinking, no one else could use that word *teleo* and mean it like Jesus did.

Then I remembered the last person that I want to look at in this chapter, Paul the apostle.

Not my will but Yours be done	▶ **Action plan** The battle of His will over ours is with us until the final exit from this world. So keep yielding yourself in surrender to the Master's will and you will succeed.

Paul the apostle

At the completion of Paul's life he uses the same word to describe the success of his life's work as Jesus did – *teleoo* – *'I ... finish my race with joy ... '*[15] And later on, the word *teleo, '... I have finished the race, I have kept the faith.'*[16] Paul followed in the footprints of Christ, a truly great, 'Completer Finisher'.

When you walk the last mile of the way on earth, resist at all costs anything that would stop you finishing your course with dignity and sweetness of spirit. Remember that none of us have ever been given a task by God that we are not capable of completing.

We are not destined for failure, but for success. How can I be so bold as to say such a thing? The answer is simple, we do not work alone, but with our Leader, who is *'The author and finisher [teleiotes] of our faith.'*[17] Here we have God the finisher, ender, perfector, completer, stepping into our weak and frail humanity to partner with us and give us victory at the end of our race.

When the explorer Alan Chambers wanted to keep his team motivated in their expedition to the North Pole, he planned a very simple incentive. On all of their clothing and equipment he had written these words, 'Keep walking'. When they drank, the words were written on the bottom of their cups for all to see. When they went to bed tired, it was on their sleeping bags. When they stumbled along the way, the message was there on their clothes and sledges ... keep walking.

The twenty-first century holds so many challenges for the Christian leader, but God who called us knows we can make it; we just have to keep walking. My prayer is that you will end your life a winner and join the other great leaders of the Bible and church history who finished well, and just kept walking.

What does it mean to finish well? It means to finish clean, with a sweet spirit, a pure love, no regrets, fulfilled, as servants and not lords, in fellowship with Christ's body, handing over a legacy of good things, surrounded with friends.

So keep walking and enjoy the final mile when it comes.

	▶ **Action plan**
The baton left and the crown received	Leave a strong baton in the hands of good leaders and walk towards the final tape with gratitude and anticipation, for your crown is secure.

Is your leadership a bottleneck to the purposes of God being fulfilled in your final mile of ministry?

1 ... 2 ... 3 ... 4 ... 5 ... 6 ... 7 ... 8 ... 9 ... 10

Notes

Chapter 1

1. Easum, Bill, 'Leadership on the Other Side', an article in the AG journal *Enrichment* (2002).
2. Neighbour, Ralph W, *Where Do We Go From Here?* (Touch Publications, 2000).
3. Hebrews 10:25.
4. Doward, Jamie, religious affairs correspondent for *The Observer*, Sunday 11 January, 2004.
5. Acts 2:42.
6. 1 Corinthians 12; Romans 8.
7. Isaiah 55:8.
8. Francis, Leslie J, *Pastoral Care Today* (Crusade for World Revival Great Britain, 2000), pp. 24–25.
9. John 4:4.
10. Acts 16:9–10.
11. Matthew 5:16.
12. Matthew 5:14–16.
13. Leadership Network, *Key Paradigm Question for Churches*, PO Box 9100, Tyler, Texas 75711-9100, 1995.

Chapter 2

1. Collins English Dictionary.
2. Hill, Phil., *The Church of the Third Millennium* (Paternoster Press, 1999), p. 3.
3. Green, Michael, *Church without Walls* (Paternoster Press, 2002), p. 105.
4. Francis, Leslie J. and Kay, William K., *Teenage Religious Values* (Gracewing, 1995), p. 79.
5. Anderson, Leith, *A Church for the 21st Century* (Bethany House Publishers, Minneapolis, 1992), p. 46.

6. Barna, George, *The Second Coming of the Church* (Word, London, 1998), p. 133.
7. Brierley, Peter, *Steps to the Future* (Scripture Press, 2000), p. 83.

Chapter 3

1. Isaiah 40:31.
2. Sample, Steven B., *The Contrarian's Guide to Leadership* (Jossey-Bass, 2002), p. 7.
3. Kahler, Martin (1908), cited by David Bosch, *Transforming Mission* (Orbis, 1992), p. 16.
4. Lings, George and Murray, Stuart, *Church Planting, Past, Present and Future* (Grove Books Ltd, 2003), p. 21.

Chapter 4

1. Wright, Walter C., *Mentoring the Promise of Relational Leadership* (Paternoster, 2004), p. xxix.
2. Harari, Oren, *The Leadership Secrets of Colin Powell* (McGraw-Hill, 2002), p. 13.
3. Matthew 28:19.
4. Matthew 28:19–20.
5. Vine, W.E., *Expository Dictionary of Bible Words* (Marshall Pickering, 1981), vol. 1, p. 316; vol. 3, p. 112.
6. Material that was gathered from 1,700 churches in the UK during the 'Jim Challenge Mission' in 1994.
7. Galatians 6:1–6.
8. Galatians 6:1–2, 4, 6.
9. Matthew 28:19.
10. The second value that Dwight Smith uses in his SCP teaching. This is also used in the first session on the 'Nature and Purpose of Church', an MA course in Mission Church run by Together in Mission in the UK.
11. Mark 16:15–18.
12. Matthew 16:18.
13. Chip R. Bell, *Mentoring as Partnership, Coaching for Leadership*, Marshall Goldsmith, Laurence Lyons and Alyssa Freas (eds.) (San Francisco: Jossey-Bass, 2000), p. 133.
14. Wright C. Walter, *Mentoring the Promise of Relational Leadership* (Paternoster, 2004), p. xviii.
15. Blanchard Ken, Miller Mark, *The Secret What Great Leaders Know and Do* (Berrett-Koehler Publishers Inc., San Francisco, 2004), p. 95.
16. Shea, Gordon F., *Making the Most of Being Mentored* (Menlo Park: Crisp Publications, 1999), p. 3.

Chapter 5
1. John 5:30.
2. World Mission Digest.
3. Hefley, James and Marti, *By Their Blood* (Baker Book House, 1996).
4. '2004 Annual Statistical Table on Global Missions' in the *International Bulletin of Missionary research* (Vol. 28, No. 1).
5. Marshall, Paul *Their Blood Cries Out* (Word Publishing, 1997).
6. Mathew 28:19–20; Mark 16:15–20; Acts 1:8.
7. Hebrews 12:2.
8. 2 Corinthians 5:10, 14–15; 2 Timothy 4.
9. Mark 6:7.
10. Acts 2:14.
11. 1 Corinthians 12:14–31.

Chapter 6
1. Smith. John S., an article entitled, 'Changemakers – Can You Trust This Man?', in *Idea* (UK Evangelical Alliance magazine, July/August 2004), p. 13.
2. Matthew 5 – 7.
3. Luke 10:18.
4. Matthew 16:23.
5. Matthew 6:33.
6. 1 Samuel 13:14.
7. 1 Corinthians 1 – 3.
8. John 13:1–17.

Chapter 7
1. 1 Corinthians 12:29.
2. 1 Corinthians 4:9; 15:9.
3. 1 Corinthians 12:28.
4. 1 Corinthians 3:4–10.
5. Ephesians 4:11.

Chapter 8
1. Acts 14:23; Titus 1:5.
2. 1 Corinthians 12 (whole chapter).
3. Ephesians 4:11; 1 Corinthians 12:28.
4. Acts 2:14.
5. Acts 2:4.
6. Acts 13:2, 5.
7. Acts 14:14.
8. Acts 9:15.
9. Ephesians 4:11.

10. Acts 18:19.
11. Acts 18:18.
12. Acts 18:27.
13. Acts 19 – 20.
14. Acts 12:17; 15:13.
15. Acts 15:22.
16. Acts 15:1–35.
17. Acts 10:1–2, 34–36, 44–47; 11:1.
18. Acts 15:22.
19. Acts 13:1.
20. Acts 14:14.
21. 1 John 2:16.
22. Song of Solomon 8:6.
23. Galatians 5:26.
24. Daniel 10:13.
25. Exodus 18:21.
26. Exodus 18:21.
27. Luke 9:22; 20:1.
28. Acts 14:12; 15:22.

Chapter 9
1. Maxwell, John, *The 21 Most Important Minutes in a Leader's Day* (Thomas Nelson Publishers, 2000), pp. 359–362.
2. Luke 6:13.
3. Matthew 28:19; Acts 6:1–7.
4. Acts 6:7.
5. Johnston, Larry, F., *The Empowered Leader* (McConkey/Johnston Inc.), p. 1.

Chapter 10
1. Traits CEOs have and will need/percent describing traits or talents dominant now in the CEO and important for the CEO of 2000. (From Lester B. Kron, *How the Next CEO Will Be Different* (Fortune, 22 May 1989), p. 175). Quoted in Quigley, p. 8.
2. Johnson, Larry, F., *Visionary Leaders* (McConkey/Johnson, Inc., Fall 2002), p. 4.
3. 1 Corinthians 14:8 (CEV).
4. Matthew 27:46.
5. 1 Corinthians 12:18.

Chapter 12
1. Matthew 25.
2. Luke 16:8.
3. Jeremiah 1:11.

4. Exodus 4:2.
5. Genesis 13:10.
6. Romans 8:38, 31; Philippians 4:13.

Chapter 13
1. Harari, Oren, *The Leadership Secrets of Colin Powell* (McGrown-Hill, 2002), p. 13.
2. Romans 12; 1 Timothy 2 – 3.
3. Acts 6:1–6.
4. 1 Timothy 3:4–5, 12; 5:17.
5. Acts 27:11; 1 Corinthians 12:28.
6. Hebrews 13:7, 17, 24.
7. Johnson, Larry, F., *Visionary Leaders* (McConkey/Johnson, Inc., Fall 2002), p. 8.
8. Matthew 5 – 7.

Chapter 14
1. 1 Samuel 3:10.
2. 1 Kings 19:11–12.
3. Matthew 5:5.
4. Psalm 138:6.
5. Acts 3 – 4.
6. *Blessed Be the Tie That Binds*, by John Fawcett.

Chapter 15
1. Matthew 15:8.
2. 1 Chronicles 16:27 (CEV).
3. 1 Timothy 1:17 (CEV).
4. Hebrews 2:9 (CEV).
5. Philippians 2:10–11.
6. John 4:44 (CEV).
7. 1 Timothy 5:17.
8. 1 Peter 3:7; Matthew 15:4.
9. Romans 12:10 (CEV).
10. 1 Corinthians 12:23 (AV).

Chapter 16
1. Acts 13:36 (AV).
2. 2 Samuel 7:4–7.
3. 1 Kings 2:10–12.
4. Joshua 1:1–9.
5. John 13:14.
6. Acts 2; 1 Corinthians 12; Romans 12.

Chapter 17

1. Exodus 40:6.
2. Zechariah 4:9.
3. Jeremiah 29:11.
4. Zechariah 4:10.
5. Zechariah 4:10.
6. Zechariah 4:6 (CEV).
7. Zechariah 4:14 (CEV).
8. Ezra 6:14.
9. 1 Kings 6:14; 9:1.
10. 1 Kings 7:1.
11. 1 Chronicles 28:21 (NIV).
12. John 4:34.
13. John 17:4.
14. John 19:30.
15. Acts 20:24.
16. 2 Timothy 4:7.
17. Hebrews 12:2.

Leadership Bottleneck Scores

We can all improve our leadership skills, so why not start with your worst performance and work every level to a better place

Chapter 1

Is your leadership a bottleneck to the new paradigm?

1 ... 2 ... 3 ... 4 ... 5 ... 6 ... 7 ... 8 ... 9 ... 10

Chapter 2

Is your leadership a bottleneck to penetrating twenty-first century culture?

1 ... 2 ... 3 ... 4 ... 5 ... 6 ... 7 ... 8 ... 9 ... 10

Chapter 3

Is your leadership a bottleneck to the thinking of your local church?

1 ... 2 ... 3 ... 4 ... 5 ... 6 ... 7 ... 8 ... 9 ... 10

Chapter 4

Is your leadership a bottleneck to core calling?

1 ... 2 ... 3 ... 4 ... 5 ... 6 ... 7 ... 8 ... 9 ... 10

Chapter 5

Is your leadership a bottleneck to mission?

1 ... 2 ... 3 ... 4 ... 5 ... 6 ... 7 ... 8 ... 9 ... 10

Chapter 6

Is your leadership a bottleneck to Kingdom living?

1 ... 2 ... 3 ... 4 ... 5 ... 6 ... 7 ... 8 ... 9 ... 10

Chapter 7

Is your leadership a bottleneck to the diversity of
gifts working together in harmony for the good of the
local church?

1 ... 2 ... 3 ... 4 ... 5 ... 6 ... 7 ... 8 ... 9 ... 10

Chapter 8

Is your leadership a bottleneck to the recognition of
'leaders of leaders'?

1 ... 2 ... 3 ... 4 ... 5 ... 6 ... 7 ... 8 ... 9 ... 10

Chapter 9

Is your leadership a bottleneck to the empowerment of
your local church for service?

1 ... 2 ... 3 ... 4 ... 5 ... 6 ... 7 ... 8 ... 9 ... 10

Chapter 10

Is your leadership a bottleneck to vision in the local church?

1 ... 2 ... 3 ... 4 ... 5 ... 6 ... 7 ... 8 ... 9 ... 10

Chapter 11

Is your leadership a bottleneck to the facilitation of other people's viewpoints and ministries?

1 ... 2 ... 3 ... 4 ... 5 ... 6 ... 7 ... 8 ... 9 ... 10

Chapter 12

Is your leadership a bottleneck to entrepreneurial contribution?

1 ... 2 ... 3 ... 4 ... 5 ... 6 ... 7 ... 8 ... 9 ... 10

Chapter 13

Is your leadership a bottleneck to good management?

1 ... 2 ... 3 ... 4 ... 5 ... 6 ... 7 ... 8 ... 9 ... 10

Chapter 14

Is your leadership a bottleneck to the practice of responsibility?

1 ... 2 ... 3 ... 4 ... 5 ... 6 ... 7 ... 8 ... 9 ... 10

Chapter 15

Is your leadership a bottleneck to the honouring factor?

1 ... 2 ... 3 ... 4 ... 5 ... 6 ... 7 ... 8 ... 9 ... 10

Chapter 16

Is your leadership a bottleneck to transitional leadership?

1 ... 2 ... 3 ... 4 ... 5 ... 6 ... 7 ... 8 ... 9 ... 10

Chapter 17

Is your leadership a bottleneck to the purposes of God being fulfilled in your final mile ministry?

1 ... 2 ... 3 ... 4 ... 5 ... 6 ... 7 ... 8 ... 9 ... 10

If you have enjoyed this book and would like to help us to send a copy of it and many other titles to needy pastors in the **Third World**, please write for further information or send your gift to:

Sovereign World Trust
PO Box 777, Tonbridge
Kent TN11 0ZS
United Kingdom

or to the '**Sovereign World**' distributor in your country.

Visit our website at **www.sovereign-world.org**
for a full range of Sovereign World books.